MATTHEW S. STANFORD, PhD, is CEO of the Hope and Healing Center & Institute (HHCI) in Houston, Texas. He is also adjunct professor of psychiatry at Baylor College of Medicine and the Houston Methodist Hospital Institute for Academic Medicine. A fellow of the Association for Psychological Science, Dr. Stanford's research on the interplay between psychology and faith has been featured in the *New York Times, USA Today, Christianity Today,* and *U.S. News & World Report.* He is the author of several books, including *Grace for the Afflicted, Grace for the Children,* and *The Biology of Sin.*

Madness and Grace

Advance Praise

"As mental health finally gains in people's awareness as a serious area of concern, here is a book that every Christian leader across the country ought to have close at hand. With a combination of clinical expertise, Christian mercy, and clear prose, Dr. Matthew Stanford walks us through the various ways that mental illness can afflict the people in our spiritual care. Not only does he present the nature of the most common disorders, we also learn to notice the red flag behaviors and indicative speech patterns that tell us when to refer to a mental health professional. *Madness and Grace* is a wise and compassionate resource that can help bring healing to countless numbers of people within the church. I highly recommend it to you!"

—**Dr. Tim Clinton**, president of the American Association of Christian Counselors

"In *Madness and Grace*, Dr. Stanford brings together the richness of his academic career and his commitment to the Christian faith to give us a thorough presentation of the mental health issues encountered by women and men in church ministries. With clarity and compassion, he guides us in how to respond to those who suffer with mental illness, as well as their families. This book should be a 'must read' for women and men preparing for ministry."

—**Nancy C. Kehoe**, RSCJ, PhD, author of *Wrestling with Our Inner Angels: Faith, Mental Illness, and the Journey to Wholeness*

"Upon finishing Dr. Stanford's outstanding work, *Madness and Grace*, one of the first words that came to mind was 'FINALLY!' For years, like many of my clergy friends, I have sought a comprehensive and thorough resource to deal with those who walk in my door seeking help, release, and support for various forms of behavioral, emotional, and mental illness. Dr. Stanford's book provides the end to that search. He shows faith leaders how they can, in fact, be the open arms of God, by revealing how faith communities can work with trained professionals in a way that puts flesh on the welcoming words, '*Come to me, all you who are weary and burdened, and I will give you rest.*' Within these pages, the reader will gain the knowledge and know-how to provide a framework of care and treatment for the one in five who suffer with some form of mental illness."

—The Reverend Dr. Russell Jones Levenson, Jr., MSTJ, Rector, Saint Martin's Episcopal Church, and Sub-Prelate, the Priory of the USA of the Order of St. John of Jerusalem

"When it comes to mental illness in America, too many people fail to get the help they need too much of the time. In *Madness and Grace*, Dr. Matthew Stanford notes how this is a divine opportunity for the church. There's a problem, however, in that clergy lack the training to help with mental illness. *When do I refer someone? How can I tell if this person is mentally ill? What should I do if someone seems suicidal?* These are the kinds of questions pastors and others in local churches ask. In this fine book, Dr. Stanford addresses these issues and teaches church leadership how to work with professionals to care for those with mental health issues. With biblical content, real-life examples, and accessible resources, Dr. Stanford offers the church a vital contribution. We can do more; *Madness and Grace* shows a way forward."

—**Ed Stetzer**, professor and dean, Wheaton College

"Mental illness continues to escalate in North America at alarming rates. For pastors and other Christ-followers who want to help mentally ill family, friends, and neighbors—and 'to do no harm'—allow me to commend this book by my friend Dr. Matthew S. Stanford. *Madness and Grace* is a rich resource for clergy and congregations who wish to serve the mentally ill looking to the Church for help and hope. One's training for ministry to the mentally ill may not end here, but I do not know of a better place to begin. I am grateful for and have benefited from this timely work and firmly believe that it will do much good for many."

—**Todd D. Still**, PhD, the Charles J. and Eleanor McLerran DeLancey Dean and the William M. Hinson Professor of Christian Scriptures, George W. Truett Theological Seminary of Baylor University

MADNESS
&
GRACE

MADNESS & GRACE

A Practical Guide for Pastoral Care and Serious Mental Illness

MATTHEW S. STANFORD, PhD

TEMPLETON PRESS

Templeton Press
300 Conshohocken State Road, Suite 500
West Conshohocken, PA 19428
www.templetonpress.org

All quotes are from the New American Standard Bible (NASB). © 1971, 1977, 1995, and 2000 by the Lockman Foundation.

Set in Garamond Premier and Tisa by Westchester Publishing Services

This paper meets the requirements of ANSI/NISO Z39.48-1992 (Permanence of Paper).

ISBN: 978-1-59947-579-0 (paperback)
ISBN: 978-1-59947-580-6 (ebook)

Library of Congress Control Number: 2021932157

A catalogue record for this book is available from the Library of Congress.

Printed in the United States of America.

21 22 23 24 25   10 9 8 7 6 5 4 3 2 1

Contents

MADNESS
&
GRACE

Introduction:
Engaging the Crisis

Madness, or what today we call serious mental illness, has been part of the human experience throughout recorded history. Families, both in the present and distant past, have struggled to understand the strange thoughts, emotions, and behaviors displayed by their afflicted loved ones. More often than not, these ill individuals and their families have been stigmatized, shamed, and mistreated by the fearful and naïve. However, one light in the dark history of madness has been the involvement of the church in the care of the broken. Long before there were effective treatments or an understanding of the role of the brain in mental illness, Christian communities stepped forward to care for the "least of these." One of the best examples of this happened in the famous *"village of lunatics,"* the Belgian town of Geel.[1]

The story of Geel (pronounced *Hyale*) begins in the seventh century with a young Irish princess named Dymphna. The daughter of Damon, a tribal king of Oriel, Dymphna and her mother were devout Christians, while her father still followed the ancient pagan rites. When Dymphna was fourteen years old, her mother suddenly died and her father was overcome by grief. As time passed, Damon sank deeper into depression over the loss of his wife, making it difficult for him to effectively rule as king. To raise his spirits, the men of his court suggested he consider a second marriage. Damon agreed on the condition that his new queen be as beautiful as his former wife. Searching throughout all of Ireland, he could find no woman as beautiful as the former queen, with the exception of Dymphna, who was the very image of her mother. Mad with grief, Damon decided that Dymphna should become his wife and take her mother's place as queen. To escape her father's sinful passions, the young princess fled during the night with her priest, Father Gerebran, and two loyal servants. Finding Dymphna gone in the morning, an enraged Damon sent his men out across the countryside to find her.

A year would pass before a small band of Damon's men, still searching for Dymphna, stopped at an inn outside the Belgian village of Geel. While paying their fees, they were intrigued to find that the innkeeper had seen their strange Irish coins before. The innkeeper explained that a group living nearby paid for goods with the same type of coins. Dymphna had been found! The men immediately sent a messenger back to Ireland to inform Damon. When the king learned of Dymphna's whereabouts, he personally traveled to Geel to retrieve his runaway daughter. Threatening Dymphna, the king commanded that she return home to become his wife or he would have Father Gerebran killed. Dymphna refused. Damon ordered his men to kill the priest in front of her. Again, Damon demanded his daughter take her mother's place as his wife, and she refused. Overcome by rage, Damon struck down the young princess with his own sword. Leaving the bodies behind, the king and his men returned to Ireland. The people of Geel buried the princess and her priest in a nearby cave.

Six hundred years later, early in the thirteenth century, excavation in and around the cave accidentally unearthed Dymphna's remains. Legend has it that several men and women suffering with madness in the area were miraculously healed upon the discovery of the grave. Word of these miraculous healings quickly spread throughout the region, and families began bringing their afflicted loved ones to pray at Dymphna's grave, with the hope that they might be healed too.

As more and more families made the pilgrimage to Geel for a miracle, the priests of nearby St. Maarten's Chapel built a shrine to hold Dymphna's relics. Dymphna was canonized by the church in 1247, and in 1349 a church honoring her was built in Geel. Within a short time, so many pilgrims were coming from across Europe to seek healing for the mentally ill that a small infirmary was built next to the church to help house them. While some did find healing, most did not. Many of the disappointed families used this opportunity to rid themselves of mentally ill relatives by leaving them at the church and returning home. It wasn't long before the sanctuary and infirmary were overflowing.

In desperation, the priests reached out to the townspeople for help. Out of charity and Christian piety, the people of Geel began taking the mentally ill into their own homes. Many of the afflicted would live out the remainder of their lives with these new families. Thus began a tradition of care that has continued for 700 years. In 1938, the community reached an all-time high when a total of 3,736 mentally ill "boarders" were placed with families in Geel. Today a modern psychiatric center sits on the site of the old infirmary next to the Church of St. Dymphna, and Geel families willing to take in a mentally ill individual have been incorporated into the modern mental health-care system. In 2019, 185 individuals were living as boarders in Geel.

If peasant farmers of the Middle Ages, empowered by their faith, could step into an impossible mental health crisis and transform tens of thousands of lives, how much more might believers do that today? The church still has a significant role in caring for those living with mental illness, and as this small Belgian town teaches us, compassion, grace, and love are powerful "treatments" it can use in such care.

MENTAL ILLNESS BY THE NUMBERS

In the United States, one out of every five adults (48 million) will experience mental illness in a given year. Perhaps a more disturbing statistic is that almost 60 percent of adults diagnosed with a mental illness receive no treatment. Ethnic minorities access mental health care at even lower rates than Caucasians (African-American, 30 percent; Hispanic, 27 percent; Asian, 18 percent; and Caucasian, 46 percent).[2]

Mental health problems also negatively impact the family and friends of the afflicted. An estimated 9 million individuals in the United States provide care for an adult with a mental illness annually. Those caregivers provide, on average, thirty-two hours of unpaid care per week. When surveyed, a vast majority of caregivers report that the situation causes them significant emotional distress, while just over half say that it has negatively impacted their own health. In addition, caring for a mentally ill loved one often results in significant financial problems for the family.[3]

THE "SYSTEM"

Our present mental health-care system is badly broken. Unlike other areas of health care, mental health care lacks a continuum of care for those needing treatment. A continuum of care is an organized system of care that moves patients, over time, through a series of health services of varying intensity. Each step in the continuum up to hospitalization represents an increase in the intensity of the services or treatments provided. The hope is that earlier steps in the process will act as a filter, minimizing the number of people that need higher levels of care. Each step in the continuum following hospitalization represents a decrease in the intensity of care, with the goal being to effectively prepare people for a return home while reducing the chances of rehospitalization for the same problem.

The table below shows that the health-care system has a well-defined continuum of care compared to the mental health-care system, which has few levels of pre-acute care, a high frequency of emergency room visits and acute hospitalizations, and no post-acute care. This has resulted in a significantly higher thirty-day rehospitalization rate for mental disorders, such as depression, bipolar disorder, and schizophrenia, compared to conditions that are unrelated to mental health.[4]

To illustrate how differently physical and mental illnesses are treated by these systems of care, let's look at two examples based on actual clinical cases.

COMPARING THE HEALTH-CARE AND MENTAL HEALTH-CARE SYSTEMS

Health-Care System	Mental Health-Care System	Phase of Care
Home Wellness/Fitness Center Pharmacy Urgent Care Primary Care Physician's Office Diagnostic Imaging Center Specialist Outpatient Procedure Center	Home Primary Care Physician's Office Mental Health-Care Provider	Pre-Acute
Emergency Room Hospitalization	Emergency Room Hospitalization	Acute
Skilled Nursing Facility Extended Care Facility Inpatient Rehabilitation Outpatient Rehabilitation Home Health Care/Hospice Home	Home	Post-Acute

Linda is a thirty-eight-year-old mother of three. She and her husband Ron have been married for ten years. For the last several days, Linda has been having indigestion and abdominal pain following meals. One morning, she stopped by the pharmacy to pick up some Pepto-Bismol after dropping her son off at kindergarten. Linda tried the over-the-counter treatment for two days, but it was ineffective. By the weekend, her symptoms included nausea, vomiting, and a low-grade fever. Ron, thinking she had a stomach bug, suggested Linda go to the local urgent-care facility. There she was given a prescription for antibiotics and an anti-nausea medication. Five days into the antibiotic treatment, her fever and vomiting were gone, but she was still having daily abdominal pain and indigestion, so she made an appointment with her primary care physician (PCP). The PCP completed a physical exam and ordered blood work. The results of the blood work showed the presence of an infection and suggested she may have a gallstone, so the PCP ordered an abdominal ultrasound and prescribed another round of oral antibiotics. The outpatient ultrasound showed inflammation of the bile duct, a stone blocking the opening of the first part of the small intestine, and significant inflammation of the pancreas. Linda was diagnosed with gallstone pancreatitis and referred to a general surgeon. The general surgeon admitted her to the hospital for a round of intravenous antibiotics before removing the gallstone and gallbladder using an open surgical procedure. Linda was in the hospital five days before she was discharged. Because a more invasive open surgical procedure was used, the surgeon requested that she have home health care for two weeks following discharge.

Linda's health-care journey started with symptoms common to many medical problems: indigestion and abdominal pain. She entered the health-care system at the pharmacy but also engaged urgent care, her PCP, a diagnostic imaging center, a surgeon, a hospital, and home health care. Her symptoms were present for two days before she went to the pharmacy and seventeen days before she was hospitalized for surgery. In total, she received thirty-four days of care, plus a follow-up appointment two weeks later with the surgeon.

Now let's look at a mental health-care example.

Tonya is a thirty-two-year-old mother of two. She and her husband Jim have been married for six years. One day, Jim came home to find that his wife had bought all new living room furniture. He was surprised she would spend so much money without consulting him. Tonya had always been very careful with the family's money. While Jim's job allowed them to live comfortably, they didn't have extra cash readily available for such an extravagant purchase without planned saving. The following day, Jim came home to find a new set of golf clubs waiting for him. He confronted Tonya about the purchases, but she said that buying things on credit was common and he should not worry about it. Tonya's spending only increased over the next two weeks. She charged both of their credit cards to the max and drained their savings. Nights were filled with Jim trying to explain to his wife the financial hole they were now in, but she seemed unconcerned. Jim also noticed that Tonya was sleeping very little and had become obsessed with keeping the "perfect" house.

Jim asked Tonya's parents to speak with her, but when they did, she again minimized the problem and said that having some debt was just the "American way." Jim also found out that the normally health conscious Tonya had started smoking. After another week of excessive spending and ever-increasing odd behavior, Jim made an appointment for him and Tonya to meet with their pastor. After listening to the couple's story, the pastor felt that the problem resulted from a lack of communication and Tonya's poor stewardship of God's financial resources. He suggested they meet with another couple in the church for marital guidance and begin attending a stewardship Bible study offered by the church. Jim and Tonya did meet with the other couple and began attending the Bible study, but things only got worse. Tonya was becoming more and more paranoid. She was absolutely convinced that Jim was having an affair with their neighbor, which caused an even greater strain on the couple's relationship. Then one afternoon Jim came home early to surprise Tonya. When she saw him, she screamed and ordered him out of the house. She ran to their bedroom, locked the door, and called 911 to report an intruder. When the police arrived, she said she did not know Jim and that he had broken into the house. After Jim proved to the police that he did indeed live there, an ambulance was called and Tonya was taken to a psychiatric hospital. She was diagnosed with bipolar disorder. After four days she was discharged to her home with a phone number for a local psychiatrist. Jim called the next day to schedule an appointment for Tonya, but the receptionist said that "due to privacy laws" Tonya would need to make her own appointment. Two days later Jim was finally able to convince Tonya to call the psychiatrist's office. She scheduled the first new-client appointment available, which was eight weeks away.

What few knew was that Tonya had suffered with significant depression at two different points during her life. The first time was when she was eighteen and went off to college. That semester, she spent most of her time in bed, failed two courses, and barely passed the others. Her parents thought it was because the high school-to-college transition had just been too difficult for a small-town girl like Tonya. By the spring semester, she returned to being her normal outgoing self.

Her second bout with depression had happened two years before, after the birth of her second child. Tonya had experienced what she assumed was the "baby blues." Her family and friends assured her it was normal, and once again, she struggled through without any mental health care. Now thirty-two, Tonya entered the mental health-care system in crisis, although the onset of her mental illness had actually begun fourteen years earlier. In women diagnosed with bipolar disorder, the first episode is most often depression rather than mania. In total, she received four days of care and a referral to a local psychiatrist.

Presently, we do not have a true mental health-care "system" in this country; instead, we have a set of disjointed mental health resources that are often difficult, if not impossible, for struggling individuals or families to locate and engage. This is not to say that psychological and psychiatric treatments do not work. Research clearly demonstrates that when individuals diagnosed with mental health conditions receive proper treatment, the vast majority show clinical improvement.[5] The problem, however, is that most individuals diagnosed with a mental illness never receive any treatment.

BARRIERS TO ACCESSING CARE

Once an individual or family attempts to engage the mental health-care system, they are confronted by obstacles that significantly hinder their ability to access services. The common barriers to accessing mental health care can be placed into three broad categories: availability, affordability, and acceptability.

Availability. There are simply not enough mental health-care providers to meet the growing demand for care. The U.S. Department of Health and Human Services estimates that a third of all U.S. residents (113 million) live in areas where there is a shortage of mental health professionals. Over half of U.S. counties have no practicing psychiatrist, while a third have no psychologist.[6] Access to care is also hindered by a serious shortage of psychiatric beds, of which fewer than one hundred thousand are available in the United States (general hospitals, 35,640; state psychiatric hospitals, 37,679; and private psychiatric hospitals, 22,020).[7] In other words, there are twenty-nine psychiatric beds for every one hundred thousand people! As a result of this lack, there are ten times more individuals with mental illness in our jails and prisons than in psychiatric hospitals. Our emergency rooms have become de facto psychiatric crisis clinics.[8] Finally, with providers and facilities being few and far between, transportation becomes a significant barrier to accessing care. In a recent survey of U.S. adults, almost half report that they or someone they know had to drive more than an hour round trip to get to their most recent mental health-care appointment.[9] For many, distance is a barrier that simply cannot be overcome.

Affordability. Cost is the primary reason that individuals report being unable to access mental health care.[10] Health insurance reimbursements to providers are far less generous for mental health conditions than for physical health issues, despite the Mental Health Parity and Addiction Equity Act signed into law by President George W. Bush in October 2008. Many health insurance policies don't even cover mental health care. This has caused many mental health providers to require payment directly from the patient rather than accept insurance. A recent study found that only

55 percent of psychiatrists accept private insurance or Medicare. Even fewer accept Medicaid (43 percent).[11] This same trend has occurred with psychologists, further limiting the mental health-care providers available to most patients.

Acceptability. Negative attitudes and beliefs toward people who suffer with mental illness are common.[12] In fact, social stigma is the second most common reason people report for not accessing mental health care. Myths—for example, that individuals with mental health problems are violent, lazy, or demon possessed—permeate our society. In a recent survey, a third of individuals with mental health problems reported worrying about others judging them, while a quarter said they had lied to avoid telling people they had sought mental health services in the past.[13]

A DIVINE OPPORTUNITY

Research over the last seven decades has consistently demonstrated that individuals in psychological distress are more likely to seek assistance from a member of the clergy before looking for help from a PCP or psychiatrist.[14] This is especially true in minority groups.[15] Viewed through the eyes of faith, it is obvious that this is not an accident but rather a divine opportunity for the church to take the lead in caring for those afflicted by mental illness.

There appear to be three main reasons that people struggling with mental health seek the assistance of clergy before other professionals. The first is ease of access. In many communities, there is a church on every corner, and these churches generally do not charge for their services. Thus barriers related to transportation and finances are removed. Second, churches are healing communities called by God to care for those in need. That's why, historically, the counsel of a wise and godly pastor has been valued in times of distress. Finally, mental illness strikes at reason and emotion—the very heart of what it is to be human. This causes most to ask the bigger questions of life such as, "Who am I?" and "Do I have value?" These are questions for which only faith has answers.

Unfortunately, a majority of clergy report feeling inadequately trained to recognize the presence of mental illness in those they counsel.[16] This is not surprising, given that few seminaries in North America provide any formal mental health training for students, despite the fact that clergy are just as likely as psychiatrists to be sought out by those with serious mental illness.[17] As a result, fewer than 10 percent of distressed individuals seeking counseling from clergy are referred to mental health professionals.[18] In addition, few faith communities offer programs, services, or resources for congregants living with mental illness, even though a majority of these individuals and their families report that they desperately want their church to be more involved in their care.[19]

PURPOSE OF THIS BOOK

The primary purpose of this book is to equip pastors, ministry staff, and lay ministers to better serve and support those suffering with mental illness who want assistance from the church. Many chapters contain a section with suggested Scripture verses and a related biblical story to assist you in ministering to individuals and families struggling with mental health problems. In addition, the book is grouped into four broad content areas, which can be called the four *R*s of mental health ministry: Recognition, Referral, Relationship, and Restoration. The four *R*s are described as follows:

1. **Recognition.** People seek the counsel of pastors for a variety of reasons, including marital discord, financial problems, and parenting issues, and it may not always be clear whether a problem stems from an underlying mental health condition. Recognizing the presence of a mental illness requires skills in psychological evaluation and assessment. While this may sound complicated, it only involves asking a simple set of standard questions that allow you to identify the person's level of psychological distress[20] and functioning as well as his or her suicidal risk.

2. **Referral**. Once you have recognized the presence of a mental health problem, it may be necessary to refer the individual to a mental health professional. The mental health-care system is complex and confusing, and few pastors have relationships with mental health-care providers beyond their local Christian counselor. To make a proper referral, you must understand the types of services that different mental health-care professionals provide. You must also build relationships with providers who are willing to collaborate with you and to promote a faith-affirming environment within their practice.

3. **Relationship**. Transformation and healing occur in supportive relationships. Unfortunately, due to stigma and misinformation, individuals living with mental illness are often isolated and alone. A supportive faith community cultivates life, while isolation brings frustration and fatigue. Actively working to break mental health–related stigma, educating your congregation, and building meaningful connections with hurting individuals and their families are important components of effective mental health ministry.

4. **Restoration**. Developing faith-based supportive services (e.g., support groups) and ministries within your church allows the individual or family seeking help to obtain some level of therapeutic care within the healing environment of the faith community itself, rather than always being sent away to get "fixed." Much like those desperate families who traveled to Geel in the Middle Ages, God is drawing those suffering with mental illness to his church, and we must be prepared to receive them.

Recognition

Understanding Mental Illness

I n a pair of highly publicized interviews in 2003 and 2005, actor Tom Cruise called psychiatry a "pseudoscience," questioned the validity of mental disorder diagnoses—specifically that of attention-deficit/hyperactivity disorder (ADHD)—and criticized actress Brooke Shields for taking psychiatric medication to treat her postpartum depression.[1] While the media suggested that Mr. Cruise's statements were driven primarily by his Scientologist beliefs, the reality is that these naïve and inaccurate opinions are common in our society. Let's look at the experience of Martin, a young man that I worked with for several years, as an illustration.

Martin has suffered with severe depression and anxiety since he was in junior high. While he did graduate from high school, his mental health problems made it impossible for him to complete college or hold a full-time job. Now twenty-three, he spends his days raising exotic plants and birds and pursuing his faith through Bible study, prayer, and volunteering at his church. While his problem symptoms are somewhat under control, due to a combination of medication and therapy, he still has intrusive thoughts of suicide on a daily basis. His unwavering pursuit of Christ, despite his prolonged and overwhelming suffering, is both heroic and inspirational.

One afternoon Martin called to ask for my advice about a conversation he'd had with his small group leader, Dan. Dan had asked him to meet that morning for coffee. During their time together, Dan shared that he had received the impression from the Holy Spirit that God wanted to heal Martin of his depression but that Martin first needed to stop taking his medication to show the "strength of his faith." To Martin, this information was both exciting and terrifying. He desperately wanted to be released from his suffering but knew the potentially lethal consequences of stopping his medication. I was filled with anger. I assured Martin that if God chose to miraculously heal his depression, he would do so, but that taking medication in no way limited or hindered the Sovereign Creator of the universe. I also told him he was one of the most godly and faithful men I knew, that his mental health problems were not the result of weak faith, and that God often chooses to use physical remedies such as medication to heal us. He wasn't completely convinced by my words but agreed not to stop taking his medication until after a period of personal prayer. I also asked him if he would allow me to talk with his small group leader about his illness. Martin was very supportive of the idea and set up a phone call between Dan and me for later that evening.

While I was angered by what Dan had said to Martin, I approached our conversation from the perspective that Dan must simply not understand the severity of Martin's illness. Dan confirmed that he had indeed told Martin to stop taking his medication and felt God wanted to bring healing to his life. I attempted to explain Martin's diagnosis and the severity of his illness. Dan's response floored me. He said, "Those diagnoses are so ill-defined and very subjective." Although he was only a recent college graduate (twenty-four years old) and had no formal training in mental health, he went on to lecture me about the uselessness of psychiatry/psychology and equated virtually all mental disorders with either personal sin or weak faith. Struggling to contain my now boiling anger, I told him that encouraging Martin to stop taking his medication would ultimately lead to his death by suicide, and I ended our conversation. Even though it was quite late in the evening, I immediately called the senior pastor of Dan and Martin's church, who, by God's providence, happened to be a long-time friend.

My friend was disturbed by what he heard. He assured me that Dan's views were not what he believed or taught and that he would immediately take care of the situation. Dan was removed as small group leader. My pastor friend met with Martin later that week, to reassure him that his illness was not the result of weak faith and that he should continue to follow his psychiatrist's instructions for taking medication. It took months for Martin to work through the trauma of that event, and a year later, he did attempt to take his life.

As this example shows, naïve and inaccurate opinions concerning mental illness are not just emotionally hurtful but have the potential to be deadly. It is important for us to recognize that those with mental illness are suffering people that God is placing in our lives. Regardless of what we may personally believe is causing their psychological distress, we must see them with the eyes of Christ and let grace be our guide.

MENTAL HEALTH/ILLNESS SPECTRUM

A mental illness, also called a mental disorder, is a disruption of a person's thoughts, moods, behavior, and/or ability to relate to others that is severe enough to require treatment or intervention. While most people experience significant changes in thoughts, moods, and relationships at some point during their lifetimes, those changes are not always severe enough to require treatment or intervention.[2] For a mental state to be classified as a disorder (or illness), it must cause dysfunction in the person's life.

The World Health Organization defines mental health as "a state of well-being in which an individual realizes his or her own abilities, can cope with the normal stresses of life, can work productively and is able to make a contribution to his or her community."[3] In other words, mental health is far more than the absence of mental illness. All people have positive and negative variations in their mental states throughout life, but only a small percentage of people are ever diagnosed with mental illness.

Given these two definitions, an individual's mental state might best be conceptualized as existing on a spectrum, with optimal mental health at one end and serious mental illness at the other (see figure below). At each moment in a person's life, his mental state falls at a point on this health/illness spectrum. Where it falls at any given time is determined by a combination of factors, including external stressors (circumstances), past experiences, ability to cope (resiliency), social support, and biology. In the figure, the widest range of mental states falls under mental health. Individuals in this part of the spectrum are dealing with zero to minimal psychological distress and flourishing in their daily lives and relationships; self-care and social support are all they require to manage stressors and problems that may arise.

The mental states between mental health and mental illness are called emotional concerns. Individuals in this range are dealing with moderate psychological distress and struggling to function normally in their daily lives and relationships. Interpersonal problems, such as marital discord or parenting difficulties, as well as subclinical mood states like "the blues" or excessive worry, might cause a person to be in this range on the spectrum. These problems are what we in mental health care refer to as "counseling issues." For a person's mental state to move from emotional concerns back into the mental health range often requires some level of professional

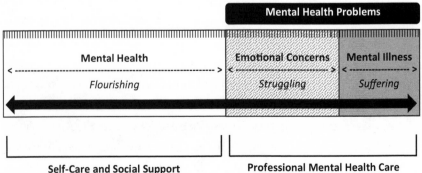

mental health care. Historically, the church has focused its resources and clergy training on this mid-level of psychological distress. In most communities, there are a number of well-trained pastoral counselors and/or licensed Christian counselors available to assist people struggling with emotional concerns.

At the far end of the spectrum, we find mental illness. An individual whose mental state falls in this range is dealing with serious psychological distress and unable to function normally in at least one area of daily life (e.g., work, school, relationships). Whether the mental state of a person suffering with mental illness will return to the healthy range of the spectrum depends on a number of factors, including the diagnosis, the level of social support available, and the type of professional mental health care received. Presently, the church lacks a meaningful and effective approach to caring for persons diagnosed with mental illness.

WHAT CAUSES A MENTAL ILLNESS?

Mental illness results from a complex interaction of biological (nature) and environmental (nurture) factors. Each of us is born with a set of biological vulnerabilities or predispositions for developing mental illness. These biological vulnerabilities are the product of our genes and neurodevelopment. Some individuals have a greater set of biological vulnerabilities than others. Having a biological predisposition toward developing a mental illness is not enough, by itself, to trigger the disorder; an individual's biological vulnerability must interact with stressful life events (e.g., poverty, abuse) to prompt the onset of the illness. The stronger a person's underlying biological vulnerability, the less stress that is needed to trigger the onset of the illness. Conversely, in individuals born with a weaker biological predisposition, greater life stress is required to produce a disorder. Until the critical level of life stress has been reached, a person generally functions normally, and her biological vulnerability remains hidden.

In addition, the balance between nature and nurture varies by mental disorder. Some mental illnesses are primarily driven by biology (e.g., schizophrenia, bipolar disorder), while others are more greatly influenced by life events (e.g., eating disorders, post-traumatic stress disorder).

COMMON RISK FACTORS

A number of developmental factors and life experiences have been shown to increase the likelihood that an individual will be diagnosed with a mental illness.[4] Prenatal risk factors include exposure to an infection or toxin in utero, maternal alcohol or drug use, maternal metabolic conditions (e.g., gestational diabetes, obesity), high levels of maternal stress, and obstetric complications. Childhood risk factors include a first-degree relative with a mental illness, a history of physical or sexual abuse or neglect, and academic failure. Life experiences shown to increase risk include major life stressors (e.g., divorce, financial problems), a chronic illness or medical condition (e.g., diabetes), a traumatic brain injury, traumatic experiences (e.g., military combat, sexual assault), substance abuse, lack of social support, and low socioeconomic status. While the presence of a single risk factor is unlikely to result in a mental illness, risk factors tend to work cumulatively in tipping the scale in the direction of a diagnosis.

HOW IS A MENTAL ILLNESS DIAGNOSED?

For the purposes of diagnosis, mental disorders have been grouped into twenty categories (e.g., Neurodevelopmental Disorders, Depressive Disorders, Obsessive-Compulsive and Related Disorders, Personality Disorders) based on their common symptoms in the *Diagnostic and Statistical Manual of Mental Disorders, Fifth Edition* (*DSM-5*), published by the American Psychiatric Association.[5] Some categories contain large numbers of disorders, while others contain few. Within each category, the criteria are listed that must be present for a person to be diagnosed with a specific mental disorder (e.g., schizoaffective disorder). In total, the *DSM-5* describes 152 specific disorders.[6]

Mental Illness and the Fall

The scriptures teach us that we live in a fallen world. The presence of illness is simply one example of the creation's brokenness. Mental illness, like all illness, is not the result of personal sin or weak faith; rather, it is evidence that we all desperately need the Savior who can heal our brokenness and make us whole.

SUGGESTED SCRIPTURES

Psalm 139:1–18   God is present with us, fully knows us, and understands our circumstances.

Romans 8:20–22   All creation is damaged by sin and longs for the day of redemption.

2 Corinthians 5:16–18   In Christ, we are a new creation, reconciled to God.

BIBLICAL STORY TO CONNECT

The Man Born Blind

John 9:1–38   Illness and disorder are an opportunity for the power of God to be displayed in our lives.

Critics of psychiatry/psychology, like Martin's small group leader Dan, argue that the diagnosis of a mental illness is too subjective and thus unreliable because mental health care as a whole lacks objective diagnostic measures (e.g., blood tests) like those used in other areas of medicine. However, the decision by a mental health professional to diagnose a person with a mental disorder is not purely subjective but rather is based on the presence of observable mood, behavioral, and cognitive criteria described in the *DSM-5*. In fact, research finds that the reliability of mental disorder diagnoses across providers is similar to diagnoses in other medical specialties such as oncology and neurology.[7]

COMMON MENTAL ILLNESSES

About half of all Americans will meet criteria for a mental disorder at some point in their life.[8] As a faith leader, you don't need to know the specific diagnostic criteria for every mental disorder, but it is important to be able to recognize signs of the most common disorders. The following section provides case examples and characteristic symptoms of the mental disorders you will most likely encounter within the church setting.

Anxiety Disorders. Affecting approximately 40 million adults yearly, anxiety disorders are the most common group of mental illnesses.[9] The characteristic symptoms of these disorders are persistent irrational fear and panic attacks. A panic attack is a distinct, overwhelming period of fear and terror in the absence of real danger. Women are twice as likely to be diagnosed with an anxiety disorder as men.[10]

WHAT TO WATCH FOR

- Excessive Worry
- Irritability/Agitation
- Problems Sleeping
- Gastrointestinal Issues
- Difficulty Concentrating
- Panic Attacks

EVELYN is a thirty-two-year-old woman who reports that she has a significant problem with worrying: "I worry all of the time and about every little thing." She reports being unable to control her worrying. This excessive and uncontrollable worry has resulted in difficulty sleeping, increased irritability with others, problems concentrating, and stomach issues. Evelyn admits that worrying has been a lifelong problem and remembers that when she was a child, her father often referred to her as a "bundle of nerves." Recently while grocery shopping, she was overcome by fear and anxiety and had to be helped by the store's staff, who called an ambulance. Evelyn meets *DSM-5* criteria for generalized anxiety disorder.

Mood Disorders. The primary mood disorders are major depressive disorder and bipolar disorder. Together, these two disorders affect approximately 25 million adults annually.[11] The main symptom of mood disorders is a chronically depressed mood or a loss of interest in previously pleasurable activities. In bipolar disorder, the depressed mood may alternate with periods of increased energy and euphoria. Mood disorders are more common in women than in men.[12]

WHAT TO WATCH FOR (DEPRESSION)

- A Persistently Sad or Empty Mood
- Feelings of Hopelessness or Worthlessness
- Frequent Minor Physical Complaints (e.g., Headaches, Stomachaches)
- Thoughts of Death or Suicide

ASHLEY is a twenty-seven-year-old woman who reports a depressed mood and a general lack of interest in activities she used to find enjoyable: "I'm concerned there might be something really wrong with me. I can't concentrate, and I often find myself crying for no reason." She reports regular dull headaches, problems sleeping, and a loss of appetite. Her extreme fatigue has caused her to miss work several times in the last few weeks. She is worried that her life will never get back to "normal" and struggles to find a reason to get up in the morning. Ashley meets the *DSM-5* criteria for major depressive disorder.

WHAT TO WATCH FOR (BIPOLAR DISORDER)

- Periods of Excessive Energy, Happiness, or Euphoria
- Extreme Religiosity

- Excessive Spending
- Promiscuity

MITCHELL is twenty-eight-year-old man who has a history of depressive episodes beginning in his late teens. He reports recently experiencing an extended period of heighted energy and mood: "It was as if I was another person. I felt like I could do anything." During this episode, he spent to excess, began abusing alcohol, and was unfaithful to his longtime girlfriend with several women. His recent extreme behavior has caused him to become alienated from his family and friends. Although he has been taking an antidepressant medication for a year, he continues to show symptoms of depression. Mitchell meets the *DSM-5* criteria for bipolar I disorder.

Substance Use Disorders. Every year approximately 19 million adults suffer with a substance use disorder.[13] The characteristic symptom of addiction is a compulsive pattern of alcohol or drug use that leads to significant impairment or distress in the individual's life. The *DSM-5* lists nine classes of substances for which substance use disorder can be diagnosed: alcohol; caffeine; marijuana; hallucinogens; inhalants; opioids; sedatives, hypnotics, or anxiolytics; stimulants; and tobacco.[14] Substance use disorders are more common in men than in women.

WHAT TO WATCH FOR

- A Decline in Physical Health
- Secrecy
- Lying and Stealing
- Irritability/Agitation
- A Lack of Personal Hygiene/Grooming
- A Sudden Change in Peer Groups
- Problems at School or on the Job
- Neglect of Relationships with Family and Friends

MILES is a fifty-eight-year-old man who reports job and relationship problems related to increased alcohol use. He states that he started drinking daily five years ago to relieve anxiety from increased job stress and marital problems, saying, "Drinking is part of my daily routine. I'm not sure I can get through the day without it." The end of his thirty-year marriage last year resulted in six months of depression and excessive drinking. His inability to perform his job during this time resulted in a demotion and required substance abuse treatment. He is highly motivated to change because he wants to rebuild his relationships with his adult children. Miles meets the *DSM-5* criteria for alcohol use disorder.

Trauma-Related Disorders. The trauma-related disorders include acute stress disorder, post-traumatic stress disorder, and adjustment disorder. Unlike other mental disorders, trauma-related disorders do not occur spontaneously but are triggered by exposure to a specific traumatic or stressful event (e.g., sexual assault, domestic violence, exposure to combat). The characteristic symptoms of the trauma-related disorders are reexperiencing the trauma through intrusive memories and nightmares, avoidance of things associated with the traumatic event, and hyperarousal.[15] Trauma-related disorders are more common in women than in men. It is estimated that over 15 million adults in the United States meet criteria for a trauma-related disorder annually.[16]

WHAT TO WATCH FOR

- Uncontrolled Thoughts or Memories of the Trauma
- Flashbacks and Nightmares
- Insomnia
- Agitation/Irritability
- Muscle Tension and Fatigue
- Sadness
- Guilt/Shame
- Anger

KIRA is a twenty-seven-year-old woman who was sexually assaulted by a stranger six months ago. She reports that she has "not been the same" since the assault and feels the experience has damaged her relationships. She says, "I never feel safe. I am constantly on guard and have trouble trusting anyone." Since the assault, she has had trouble sleeping and reports being easily startled by noise. She describes having intrusive memories about the trauma on a daily basis. In an attempt to minimize these painful thoughts, she avoids contact with others and has been isolating herself at home. When she does interact with others, she is easily agitated and often snaps at people. Kira meets *DSM-5* criteria for post-traumatic stress disorder.

Eating Disorders. Approximately 2 million adults suffer with an eating disorder in the United States every year.[17] The *DSM-5* lists criteria for three eating disorder diagnoses: anorexia nervosa, bulimia nervosa, and binge eating disorder. All of the eating disorders are characterized by an unhealthy preoccupation with weight, body shape, and food, leading to dangerous eating behaviors. Eating disorders are far more common in women than in men.[18]

WHAT TO WATCH FOR

- Fainting
- Hair Loss
- Hoarding of Food
- Tooth Erosion
- Gastrointestinal Problems
- Dramatic Weight Changes
- Compulsive Food/Eating Rituals
- An Obsessive Preoccupation with Weight Gain

MARIA is a seventeen-year-old woman referred by her parents, who are concerned she may be developing an eating disorder. Ordinarily an active teen of normal weight, she has gained more than forty pounds since her freshman year in high school. For the past year she has struggled with depression, and recently she fainted at school during her physical education class. Her parents report that she has stopped eating dinner with the family and spends most of her time alone in her bedroom. They became concerned about an eating disorder when they found a large plastic tub of junk food hidden in Maria's closet. Maria meets *DSM-5* criteria for binge eating disorder.

Psychotic Disorders. The characteristic symptom of the psychotic disorders is a break with reality that manifests as delusions (believing something to be true that is not) and/or hallucinations (perceiving things that are not truly present).[19] Schizophrenia is the most common of the psychotic disorders. It is estimated that 1.3 million adults in the United States suffer with a psychotic disorder every year. These disorders affect men and women equally.[20]

WHAT TO WATCH FOR

- Paranoia
- Isolation/Withdrawal
- Confusion
- Difficulty Concentrating
- Extreme Religiosity
- Disorganized Thinking and Behavior
- The Perception of Voices Speaking
- A Limited Range of Emotions
- Strange and Extreme Beliefs

CONNOR is a twenty-one-year-old man in his second year of college who reports a persistent fear that the federal government has him under surveillance. He insists that problems with his Wi-Fi connection and a higher-than-normal electric bill are evidence of hidden surveillance devices in his apartment. He recently stopped attending class because he feared he was being followed by government agents. This caused his roommates to become concerned, and they contacted his parents. "I wish people would listen to me," he says. "I'm not crazy. This is really happening." He reports that he often stays up all night watching movies on Netflix, through which he receives information that helps him understand the government's secret plans. Connor meets *DSM-5* criteria for schizophrenia.

HOW ARE MENTAL ILLNESSES TREATED?

Mental disorders are chronic and recurrent conditions that we presently cannot cure. Their treatment—similar to that of other chronic conditions, such as type 1 diabetes, asthma, and hypertension—amounts to symptom management. While a majority of patients receive treatment through mental health services delivered in outpatient settings, mental illness can sometimes become so severe that an individual requires admittance to a psychiatric hospital. This occurs when a patient becomes unable to care for himself properly or when there is an immediate danger of suicide or harm to others. Today, virtually all inpatient psychiatric care is for acute crisis intervention. The average length of stay for patients with a mental disorder diagnosis in the United States is only six days.[21] However, little more than stabilization is possible in such a short period. Conversely, a comprehensive and effective approach to treating mental illness includes four major components: psychiatric medication, psychotherapy, healthy lifestyle changes, and social support.

Psychiatric Medication. The primary purpose of psychiatric medication is to minimize the symptoms of a mental illness by altering the way brain cells (neurons) communicate with one another. Unfortunately, these medications often have troublesome side effects, such as constipation, dry mouth, drowsiness, weight gain, and irritability. While psychiatric medications can greatly improve a person's quality of life by managing problem symptoms, they are not a cure. The most commonly prescribed psychiatric medications fall into five classes: stimulants, antidepressants, antipsychotics, mood stabilizers, and anxiolytics (see table below).

CLASSES OF COMMON PSYCHIATRIC MEDICATIONS

Medication Class	Condition Prescribed For	Common Brand Names
Stimulants	Attention-Deficit/ Hyperactivity Disorder	Adderall, Ritalin, Vyvanse
Antidepressants	Major Depressive Disorder Anxiety Disorders	Prozac, Wellbutrin, Zoloft
Antipsychotics	Psychotic Disorders	Abilify, Risperdal, Seroquel
Mood Stabilizers	Bipolar Disorder	Depakote, Lamictal, Lithium
Anxiolytics	Anxiety Disorders	Ativan, Klonopin, Xanax

Psychotherapy. During psychotherapy (also called talk therapy), a client and therapist meet regularly in private sessions to talk about concerns and issues related to the client's mental illness. The goal of this therapy is to help clients better regulate their thinking and emotional responses to stressful situations, understand how their mental disorders affect their daily lives, and learn ways to manage problem symptoms. Various psychotherapeutic approaches have been shown to be effective, including cognitive-behavioral therapy (CBT) (used to treat multiple mental disorders), exposure therapy (to treat phobias, social anxiety disorder, and PTSD), dialectical behavior therapy (DBT) (to treat borderline personality disorder, suicidal behavior, and substance use disorders), and motivational enhancement therapy (MET) (to treat substance use disorders). Psychotherapy can be done with an individual or family, or in a group setting.

Healthy Lifestyle Changes. Keeping the body (including the brain) healthy helps lessen the severity of symptoms related to a mental disorder. In addition, healthy lifestyle changes help offset the problem side effects of psychiatric medications (e.g., weight gain). Healthy lifestyle changes needed by those undergoing psychiatric treatment can include sleeping well, eating healthier, becoming more active, getting involved in pleasurable mental activities (e.g., reading), and developing an active spiritual life.

Social Support. Research has consistently shown that social support is a key component of strong mental health.[22] Social support contributes to the treatment of those with mental disorders by reducing isolation, encouraging healthy choices and behaviors, promoting the development of positive coping skills, improving motivation, and providing a sense of belonging. Social support may be provided by family, friends, a support group, or the church.

RECOVERY

Research shows that recovery and remission are possible for those with mental illness.[23] In fact, a majority of people diagnosed with mental disorders, if properly treated, will recover to the point that they reengage in their community and live meaningful, happy lives. As a faith leader, your job is not to "fix" those struggling with mental illness but simply to relieve their psychological suffering when possible, while revealing the unconditional love and limitless grace that is available only through a personal relationship with Jesus Christ.

That is exactly what Pastor Mark and the congregants of his small Bible Church did when they encountered a homeless woman struggling with trauma-related mental health problems. Over a series of several mornings, Mark had arrived at the church office early and noticed a small pickup truck in the parking lot. He didn't think much of it, because the truck was always gone soon afterward. Then one morning the driver, Deborah, approached Mark and asked if he could give her truck a jumpstart. As he helped her, Mark learned that Deborah was homeless and living in her vehicle. She had been staying in the church's parking lot most nights over the last two weeks. During the day she would drive around looking for work in the area. He suggested a local shelter, but Deborah did not feel those places were safe for women and preferred to sleep in her truck. So Mark told her that she was welcome to continue staying in the church's parking lot at night. Over the next several months, Mark and the congregants of the church began to help Deborah in ways that made her daily life easier and facilitated her efforts to find a job. They bought gas and tires for her truck, paid her cell phone bill, provided food, and gave her access to the church's kitchen and bathroom during the day. Deborah began attending the church's Sunday morning worship service and, over time, a weekly Bible study at a congregant's home. Mark said, "The church was very accepting of Deborah. They loved her well." After working several short-term jobs lasting only a few days, Deborah was finally able to find permanent employment and no longer had to live in her truck. While Pastor Mark and the congregation never directly engaged Deborah's mental health problems, they were able to minimize her psychological distress and improve her quality of life.

Evaluation and Assessment

Oscar and his wife, Doris, have faithfully served as missionaries to Africa for over thirty years. Recently their mission organization increased the required fundraising goals for all missionaries. Unfortunately, this came at a time when Oscar was seeing a drop in his annual support. Falling short of his required funding goals caused Oscar significant anxiety. He ignored the problem until the mission organization brought it to his attention. Oscar and his wife were required to attend a conference aimed at assisting missionaries who had not met their fundraising goals.

While at the conference, Oscar's anxiety became so intense that he experienced a panic attack. At the time, however, Doris believed he was suffering a stroke, because his speech became slurred and he was disoriented. He was taken to a hospital by ambulance, and following an evaluation, it was determined that he had not suffered a stroke. Oscar returned home, but he continued to experience anxiety, feeling he was being scrutinized by the organization. As a result, he became extremely depressed. Thinking the problem was primarily spiritual in nature, the couple approached a local pastor for counseling.

Over the following weeks, Oscar became increasingly paranoid and delusional. He started to believe that the mission organization had hidden cameras in his home and was watching him. To avoid their surveillance, he would drive around all day and night, eventually sleeping in the car because he was afraid to go home. This led to Oscar being hospitalized for a week at a psychiatric facility. After discharge, he was referred to a psychiatrist who prescribed medication. Initially, he was not willing to take the medication, but after consulting with the pastoral counselor, he agreed to the treatment. After several sessions of pastoral counseling, Oscar was referred to a clinical psychologist for therapy. At first, Oscar and his wife were resistant to the idea of therapy. They were concerned that "secular therapy" might contradict and invalidate their faith. After the pastor explained that he and the psychologist would be working collaboratively, however, Oscar agreed to the treatment. It was important to Oscar and his wife that their faith be not only respected but also used throughout the treatment process. Had this collaborative approach not been available, Oscar would not have engaged in therapy.

After the first therapy session, the psychologist was contacted by Oscar's pastoral counselor via email. They agreed that the psychologist would focus on Oscar's depression and anxiety symptoms, using cognitive-behavioral therapy, while the pastor would focus on helping Oscar to understand and rely on God's compassionate and loving character in difficult experiences. They also agreed to discuss the case weekly over the phone. The weekly call allowed the pastoral counselor to inform the therapist of psychological concerns raised by Oscar (e.g., memory problems), while the psychologist was able to update the pastoral counselor on spiritual issues that Oscar was struggling with. After fourteen weeks of collaborative treatment, Oscar's depression and anxiety symptoms had become minimal and well managed, so they decided he would continue to meet weekly only with his pastoral counselor and participate in a faith-based mental health support group. Oscar would have a follow-up visit with the psychologist in one month.

GUIDING PRINCIPLES

Within the church setting, pastoral counselors are presented with a wide variety of distressing problems and issues by congregants desperately seeking guidance and support. Pastoral counseling concerns include marriage and family issues (e.g., domestic abuse, parenting, infidelity, divorce), financial problems (e.g., unemployment, poverty, excessive spending), spiritual issues (e.g., dreams/visions, sin, spiritual direction, faith crises), grief/loss (e.g., a loved one's death, the diagnosis of a serious medical condition), relational problems (e.g., unresolved conflict, guilt, anger), addiction (e.g., alcohol, drugs, pornography, overeating), and emotional challenges (e.g., depression, anxiety). Recognizing the presence of a mental illness within this vast collection of emotional pain and suffering is not always easy. In fact, all of the problems just mentioned can lead to or be symptomatic of a mental disorder.

While a vast majority of clergy report feeling inadequately trained to recognize the presence of mental illness in congregants who approach them for counseling,[1] my experience working with pastors suggests that the issue is actually more of feeling inadequately trained to provide a diagnosis. Providing a psychiatric diagnosis, however, should not be an expectation of the clergy. On the other hand, while a church is not generally viewed as a clinical setting, those involved in pastoral counseling must be equipped to recognize the potential presence of an underlying mental health problem that requires referral to a mental health-care provider. This does not mean that the spiritual counsel and guidance offered by a pastoral counselor is not of value. It does mean that, as in Oscar's case, where a mental disorder is present, a more collaborative approach to care, which includes both spiritual counsel and professional mental health treatment, is needed.

Simply recognizing symptoms can be quite easy; a pastor need follow only two guiding principles, using a semistructured approach to obtain information about the counselee and his problem during the initial meeting. The first guiding principle is simply to be aware. Remember, research shows that individuals in psychological distress are more likely to go to clergy *before* going to a physician or mental health-care provider.[2] As such, the distressed person who has sought your counsel may not know that he is struggling with a mental health problem and is thus unlikely to describe it in those terms (although in some cases he might). So keep an open mind and don't jump to conclusions. Marital discord, financial issues, or parenting problems may not be what they appear; the issue being discussed may only be a symptom of a larger disorder (e.g., excessive spending can be a symptom of mania in bipolar disorder).

The second guiding principle for an effective evaluation is to think holistically. God has created each person as a complex union of physical and nonphysical facets. Specifically, there are four facets of the self, which perhaps are most clearly outlined in Luke 2:52. Describing the development of the young Christ, Luke writes, "Jesus kept increasing in wisdom [mental] and stature [physical], and in favor with God [spiritual] and men [relational]." Jesus also outlined these four facets when, quoting Deuteronomy 6:5, he said, "Love the Lord your God with all your heart [mental/emotional] and with all your soul [spiritual] and with all your mind [mental/rational] and with all your strength [physical] ... [and] Love your neighbor as yourself [relational]" (Mark 12:30–31). We, like the incarnate Christ, are a unity of physical, mental, spiritual, and relational facets, with each aspect affecting and being affected by all the others. We are far more complex than a spirit trapped inside a physical body.

Therefore, when working with those in distress, remove your spiritual blinders. Do not overspiritualize their problems (e.g., do not consider symptoms of an anxiety disorder a sign of distrust in God or auditory hallucinations evidence of demonic possession) but view people and their problems holistically. Ask how the issue affects a person at each level of being: physically, mentally, spiritually, and relationally. Since God has made each of us a unity of these facets, each facet is important in helping to identify the cause of the problem, the level of dysfunction, and the process necessary for recovery.

The Church Is a Healing Community

God has called us, as the church, to care for the sick. In fact, we are told that when we care for the "least of these," it is as if we are doing it for Christ. For those struggling with mental illness, the church should be an accessible and welcoming starting point on the path to healing.

SUGGESTED SCRIPTURES

Proverbs 19:20   We are called to seek out godly counsel.

John 10:20   Jesus understands the stigma and shame associated with mental illness.

James 5:14–15   The church is a place for physical and spiritual healing.

BIBLICAL STORY TO CONNECT

The Good Samaritan

Luke 10:30–37   As Christ followers, we should seek to lessen the suffering of our "neighbor" whenever possible.

ASSESSMENT QUESTIONS

There are four situations in which you should refer someone to a licensed mental health-care provider: when the individual is (1) experiencing delusions and/or hallucinations, (2) actively misusing alcohol and/or drugs, (3) displaying a significant level of psychological distress (suggesting the presence of an untreated mental disorder), or (4) in danger of harming himself or others.

The following sections contain questions you can ask to help you determine whether to make a referral to a mental health-care professional. (Although note that the process for assessing suicidal risk will be discussed in a later chapter.) These questions can also help give direction to the discussion and possibly guide you toward more definitive next steps. While you should try your best to adhere to the suggested questions, asking additional questions, as needed, for clarification and follow topical trajectories in the conversation is encouraged when you feel it is appropriate.

Primary Complaint or Concern. Of course, the first course of action is to determine the primary complaint or concern that has brought the individual to pastoral counseling. Once that has been defined, use the following questions to help the counselee elaborate on her primary complaint, especially in relation to the issue's onset, progress, and level of impairment.

1. When did this problem/concern begin?
2. How has the problem progressed? For example, have there been times when the issue became better or worse?
3. Does the problem interfere with your ability to go to work or school or to maintain healthy relationships? Impairment in at least one area of daily function is often symptomatic of a mental health problem.

Mental Health History. A brief history of past mental health problems and interventions can provide insight into the person's present complaint. The following questions will help you gather information on the individual's previous interactions with the mental health-care system. The recurrence of a mental health problem that required professional care in the past suggests that a referral may be in order.

1. Have you ever had the same problem or a similar concern in the past? If yes, what did you do to resolve it?
2. Have you ever seen a counselor or other mental health-care professional? If yes, for what?

3. Have you ever taken medication for a mental health problem? If yes, which medication(s)?

4. Have you ever been hospitalized for a mental health problem? If yes, how long ago?

Presence of Delusions and Hallucinations. The occurrence of delusional thinking or hallucinations is evidence of a profound distortion in a person's perception of reality. Delusions are false beliefs that a person holds strongly despite being presented with clear evidence to the contrary. The most common delusional themes are presented in the table below.

COMMON DELUSIONAL THEMES

Theme	False Belief
Persecution	The belief that he is being or will be harmed or harassed by another.
Religion	A preoccupation with extreme religious experiences and beliefs.
Reference	Certain gestures, comments, or environmental cues are directed at you.
Grandiosity	The impression that she has exceptional abilities, wealth, or fame.
Erotomania	The belief that another person is in love with him.
Nihilism	The idea that a major catastrophe will soon occur.
Somatic Issues	A preoccupation with one's health and organ function.

Hallucinations are sensory experiences in which the person reports seeing, hearing, smelling, tasting, or feeling something that is not actually present. For example, auditory hallucinations are most commonly described as "hearing voices" that are distinct from one's thoughts.

Since the person fully accepts that these false beliefs or experiences are true, she may appear very confident and rational when discussing them. If you are concerned that an individual may be experiencing delusions or hallucinations, ask the following questions to help make that determination.

1. Do you ever hear things that other people don't hear or see things that other people don't see?
2. Do you feel that someone is watching you or trying to hurt you?
3. Do you have any special abilities or powers?

Use of Alcohol and Drugs. Regardless of the person's primary complaint or concern, you should always screen for the misuse of alcohol and drugs. In a recent LifeWay Research study, slightly more than half (52 percent) of Protestant pastors surveyed reported personally knowing someone in their congregations who was struggling with opioid abuse.[3] Almost half (47 percent) of individuals diagnosed with a substance use disorder also meet criteria for a coexisting mental illness.[4] It is important to rule out alcohol and substance misuse as the underlying cause of or contributor to the person's primary complaint. Start with three general questions to determine the person's pattern of use.

1. Do you enjoy a drink now and then? If yes, how often?
2. Have you used drugs, including prescription drugs, in the past year? If yes, which drugs?
3. Has this problem/concern caused you to drink or use drugs more often than usual?

Given that the abuse of alcohol and misuse of drugs is generally looked down upon, it is possible that the counselee may be guarded or resistant to answering these questions. If so, move on to the psychological distress section and come back to these questions at the end of the assessment. If the counselee is never willing to answer the questions, you should assume that they are struggling with a substance abuse problem.

On the other hand, if answers to the above questions reveal that an individual has increased alcohol or drug use in an attempt to manage distress, this is a troubling sign that suggests the individual is overwhelmed and unable to cope with problems in a healthy way. At this point, a pattern of use has been established, so move on to the following four yes/no questions to screen for misuse. If the individual answers positively (yes) to one or more of the following questions, substance abuse is likely present.[5]

1. Have you ever felt that you ought to cut down on your drinking or drug use?
2. Have people annoyed you by criticizing your drinking or drug use?
3. Have you ever felt bad or guilty about your drinking or drug use?
4. Have you ever had a drink or used drugs first thing in the morning to steady your nerves or to get rid of a hangover?

Level of Psychological Distress. Psychological distress is a general term used to describe unpleasant feelings or emotions that negatively impact an individual's level of functioning. Characterized by depression and anxiety symptoms, psychological distress is emotional discomfort that interferes with the normal activities of daily living. Significantly high levels of psychological distress indicate the presence of a mental disorder. A simple yet accurate measure of psychological distress that you can easily administer in an interview format is the six-item Kessler Scale of Unspecified Psychological Distress (K6).[6] Counselees answer the questions based on their feelings over the past thirty days, scoring each question with a number from 0 to 4 using the following scale: all of the time (4 points), most of the time (3 points), some of the time (2 points), a little of the time (1 point), or none of the time (0 points).

1. How often during the past thirty days did you feel **nervous?**
2. During the past thirty days, how often did you feel **hopeless?**
3. During the past thirty days, how often did you feel **restless or fidgety?**
4. During the past thirty days, how often did you feel **so depressed that nothing could cheer you up?**

5. During the past thirty days, how often did you feel **that everything was an effort**?

6. During the past thirty days, how often did you feel **worthless**?

Once the questions are answered, add up the points to obtain a total score. Total scores on the K6 can range from 0 to 24. Scores are interpreted as follows: 0–2 = no psychological distress, 3–5 = mild psychological distress, 6–9 = moderate psychological distress, and 10–24 = severe psychological distress. Individuals displaying severe psychological distress are likely to meet *DSM-5* criteria for a mental disorder and should be referred to a licensed mental health-care provider.

CASE EXAMPLES

The following case examples show how you might use the screening questions to assess the need for a referral to a mental health provider.

CASE EXAMPLE 1. Mark is a successful thirty-two-year-old financial advisor who has come for pastoral counseling because he feels down most of the time. His wife suggested he seek help after she found him crying at home over the weekend. Mark came to know Christ through a college ministry when he was twenty-one. He and his wife Jane have been married for five years and have a two-year-old son, Ryan. They have been members of the church for the past three years. Mark is involved in the men's group and serves as an usher some Sundays. Jane attends the women's Bible study and takes advantage of the church's mother's day out program for Ryan.

Primary Complaint or Concern

Mark, I'd like to ask you a series of questions to help me better understand your struggles and to help us find the best course of action. When did this problem begin?

▶ "About two months ago. I started having thoughts that I'm not good enough at my job, not a good enough husband, not a good enough father, not a good enough Christian. At this point, I feel totally worthless. Maybe I just don't appreciate all that God has given me."

How have these thoughts of worthlessness progressed over the last two months? Have there been times when such thinking became better or worse?

▶ "It has been mostly a downhill slide for the past two months. Occasionally, I'll have a good moment and start to feel better, but it never lasts more than an hour or so."

Has this interfered with your ability to work or maintain healthy relationships?

▶ "I've missed a lot of work in the last month. I have trouble sleeping, so I'm exhausted most of the time. I'm waking up in the middle of the night and can't stop thinking about all the ways I've let my family or God down. Some mornings I just can't get myself up and go to work. When I do go to work, I'm distracted at the office and feel inadequate. My job performance has clearly suffered as a result. At home, I avoid Jane, because when we do interact, I snap at her or blow up. I feel so disconnected from God. It's almost impossible for me to pray. I haven't opened my Bible or attended Sunday service in over a month."

Mental Health History

Have you ever had the same or a similar issue in the past?
▶ "No, I've always considered myself an upbeat, happy guy."

Have you ever seen a counselor or other mental health-care professional?
▶ "No."

Have you ever taken medication for a mental health problem?
▶ "No."

Presence of Delusions and Hallucinations

Since Mark does not display any delusional thinking or report hallucinations it is not necessary to ask him this set of questions.

Use of Alcohol and Drugs

Do you enjoy a drink now and then? If yes, how often?
▸ "We do have wine with dinner a few times a week, and I will have a margarita on occasion when we go out for Mexican food."

Have you used drugs, including prescription drugs, in the past year?
▸ "No."

Have these thoughts and feelings of worthlessness caused you to drink more often than usual?
▸ "I'm embarrassed to say that it has. I drink a glass or two of wine a day now, just to try and quiet down the incessant thoughts of worthlessness."

Have you ever felt that you ought to cut down on your drinking?
▸ "I have thought that recently."

Have people annoyed you by criticizing your drinking?
▸ "No."

Have you ever felt bad or guilty about your drinking?
▸ "Absolutely! I've become so weak that I need wine to get through a day. Just another example of what a failure I am."

Have you ever had a drink first thing in the morning to steady your nerves or to get rid of a hangover?
▸ "No."

Level of Psychological Distress

I'm going to ask you some questions, and I'd like you to answer them based on how you have felt over the last thirty days. First, how often during the past

*thirty days have you felt **nervous?** Would you say all of the time (4), most of the time (3), some of the time (2), a little of the time (1), or none of the time?*
▸ "Most of the time." [3 points]

*During the past thirty days, how often did you feel **hopeless?** All of the time (4), most of the time (3), some of the time (2), a little of the time (1), or none of the time (0)?*
▸ "All of the time." [4 points]

*During the past thirty days, how often did you feel **restless or fidgety?** All of the time (4), most of the time (3), some of the time (2), a little of the time (1), or none of the time (0)?*
▸ "None of the time." [0 points]

*During the past thirty days, how often did you feel **so depressed that nothing could cheer you up?** All of the time (4), most of the time (3), some of the time (2), a little of the time (1), or none of the time (0)?*
▸ "All of the time." [4 points]

*During the past thirty days, how often did you feel **that everything was an effort?** All of the time (4), most of the time (3), some of the time (2), a little of the time (1), or none of the time (0)?*
▸ "Most of the time." [3 points]

*During the past thirty days, how often did you feel **worthless?** All of the time (4), most of the time (3), some of the time (2), a little of the time (1), or none of the time (0)?*
▸ "All of the time." [4 points]

MARK'S MENTAL HEALTH RED FLAGS

- He had a clear change from his normal mood two months ago.
- He has experienced a persistent, progressive decline since then.
- There has been a negative impact on his job performance and marriage.
- He has increased his alcohol use to cope.

■ His K6 score of 18 points shows he is experiencing severe psychological distress.

While continued pastoral counseling that focuses on his identity and value in Christ would be beneficial, a referral to a mental health-care provider is strongly suggested.

CASE EXAMPLE 2. Jess is a twenty-two-year-old part-time college student brought in by her parents because of her increasingly odd behavior. They report that over the past several weeks, she has stopped going to work and school, stays out late partying, sleeps most of the day, and often talks loudly to herself in her room, as if arguing with someone. These are all significant changes from how she was just a month ago. Then three days ago, they decided to seek help after Jess moved her bed into the closet in her room and started sleeping there. When they asked her why she was sleeping in the closet, she simply said, "You wouldn't understand." Jess refused to see a physician but did agree to speak with a pastor. Jess's parents have been active members of the church for over twenty-five years. Jess was actively involved in the youth group during high school but has attended Sunday services only sporadically since graduating.

Primary Complaint or Concern

Jess, I'd like to ask you a series of questions to help me better understand your present struggles and help us find the best course of action. Tell me what's going on.
❱ "Nothing. My parents just don't understand me, so they think I'm crazy. They wanted me to go see a doctor, but I'd rather talk to you. At least you understand spiritual issues."

What don't they understand about you?
❱ "They don't understand that I'm finally going to live my own life. Be my own person. I'm an adult and I can make my own decisions. You'd think they would be happy for me."

Is that why you stopped going to work and school?
▶ "Yes. I have bigger plans than a dead-end job and junior college."

Tell me about your plans.
▶ "I can't tell you."

Why?
▶ "It would only confuse you. You wouldn't understand."

Why wouldn't I understand?
▶ "It's not your fault. You haven't been enlightened like I have."

Your parents say it sometimes sounds like you're arguing with someone in your room. Can you tell me about that?
▶ "I wish I could tell you, but I can't. Like I said, it would only confuse you. It is important that I make things more peaceful, not more chaotic. I wish someone else could understand. But I know that in the end it will be the best thing for the world. My parents should be happy that I have finally found my purpose for living. They should be more supportive and stop trying to stop me."

Mental Health History

Have you ever seen a counselor or other mental health-care professional?
▶ "No! So you think I'm crazy too! I thought you would be different. You're just like everyone else."

Have you ever taken medication for a mental health problem?
▶ "No!"

Presence of Delusions and Hallucinations

Do you ever hear things that other people don't hear or see things that other people don't see?
▶ "I only hear and see what I am supposed to hear and see. If others can't hear and see what I do, that's their problem, not mine."

Do you feel that someone is watching you or trying to hurt you?

❯ "Absolutely, and my parents are part of it. They all want to stop me from becoming who I have been called to be. But I know who they are, and I will not be stopped."

Is that why you are sleeping in your closet?

❯ "Yes. They cannot see my dreams when I sleep in there. Everything is clear in my dreams. The Bible talks a lot about dreams."

Who can't see your dreams?

❯ "I can't tell you. If you speak their names, they know where you are."

Do you have any special abilities or powers?

❯ "Only the abilities that they have given me so that I might become who I am supposed to be. You'll all understand soon enough."

Who gave you these abilities?

❯ "I can't tell you, but don't worry, they are good."

Use of Alcohol and Drugs

Do you enjoy a drink now and then?

❯ "I'm twenty-two years old! I can drink when I want. You're just like my parents."

Have you used drugs, including prescription drugs, in the past year?

❯ "I'd rather not say."

Have you ever felt that you ought to cut down on your drinking?

❯ [No answer.]

Have people annoyed you by criticizing your drinking?

❯ "My parents won't get off my case about it. So, I have a few drinks. So what?"

Have you ever felt bad or guilty about your drinking?

❯ "Never. Why should I? Jesus turned water into wine."

Have you ever had a drink or used drugs first thing in the morning to steady your nerves or to get rid of a hangover?

❱ "No."

Level of Psychological Distress

*I'm going to ask you some questions, and I'd like you to answer them based on how you have felt over the last thirty days. First, how often during the past thirty days have you felt **nervous?** Would you say all of the time (4), most of the time (3), some of the time (2), a little of the time (1), or none of the time?*

❱ "A little of the time." [1 point]

*During the past thirty days, how often did you feel **hopeless?** All of the time (4), most of the time (3), some of the time (2), a little of the time (1), or none of the time (0)?*

❱ "None of the time." [0 points]

*During the past thirty days, how often did you feel **restless or fidgety?** All of the time (4), most of the time (3), some of the time (2), a little of the time (1), or none of the time (0)?*

❱ "Some of the time." [2 points]

*During the past thirty days, how often did you feel **so depressed that nothing could cheer you up?** All of the time (4), most of the time (3), some of the time (2), a little of the time (1), or none of the time (0)?*

❱ "None of the time." [0 points]

*During the past thirty days, how often did you feel **that everything was an effort?** All of the time (4), most of the time (3), some of the time (2), a little of the time (1), or none of the time (0)?*

❱ "None of the time." [0 points]

*During the past thirty days, how often did you feel **worthless?** All of the time (4), most of the time (3), some of the time (2), a little of the time (1), or none of the time (0)?*

❱ "None of the time." [0 points]

JESS'S MENTAL HEALTH RED FLAGS

- She has displayed increasingly odd behavior over the past month.
- She experiences paranoid delusional thinking.
- She reports having auditory hallucinations (hearing voices).
- There has been a negative impact on her job and her school performance.
- She is defensive about her alcohol use.

Jess is clearly guarded and not being fully cooperative. She appears to be actively abusing alcohol and possibly drugs. Jess's mental health is clearly deteriorating, and she seems to be on the verge of a mental health crisis. Given that she is in the age range for the onset of the psychotic disorders (e.g., schizophrenia), her parents should be encouraged to immediately take her to a mental health crisis clinic or hospital emergency room. Stabilization will likely require a short period of inpatient hospitalization. Once Jess has received psychiatric treatment, pastoral counseling may be useful to help her differentiate between genuine religious and spiritual experiences and those caused by mental illness. Given Jess's resistance to treatment, it would be best to discuss any recommendation for care with her parents first and then collaboratively develop a plan with them on how to present this information to her.

BURDEN BEARING

While an important part of pastoral care is knowing when to make a referral for an underlying mental health problem, the primary goal must always be to help the counselee feel heard and understood in relation to his concern.

God has called us to "bear one another's burdens" (Gal. 6:2), because finding someone who will truly listen and empathize with your burden can be transformative in and of itself. People often wait until their suffering is so great that it outweighs the fear, mistrust, or embarrassment that previously prevented them from seeking help. So it is possible that you will be meeting people at some of the worst points in their lives. Be willing to step into their pain and to help bear their burdens.

When working with those in severe psychological distress, compassion and grace are always the first line of pastoral care. Mental health planning and treatment come second.

Child and Adolescent Mental Health

In the United States, one out of every five children ages three to seventeen years old (17 million) will experience mental illness in a given year. While mental illness is thought of primarily as a problem of adulthood, the reality is that half of all lifetime mental disorders begin by the age of fourteen, while 75 percent begin by age twenty-four.[1] The average delay between the onset of symptoms and the first treatment is eleven years.[2] Sadly, 50 percent of children diagnosed with a mental illness never receive the necessary treatment for their condition.[3] When left untreated, mental health problems can lead to serious, even life-threatening, consequences. Suicide, for which mental illness is a major precipitating factor, is now the second leading cause of death among youth aged ten to nineteen years old.[4]

COMMON CHILDHOOD MENTAL DISORDERS

A quarter of the youth diagnosed with mental disorders show serious functional impairment, meaning their mental health problem significantly interferes with or limits one or more major life activities (e.g., school).[5] So as a pastoral counselor, it is important that you become familiar with the most common childhood mental disorders. The following section provides case examples and lists the characteristic symptoms of the childhood mental disorders that you will most likely encounter within the church setting.

Attention-Deficit/Hyperactivity Disorder. An estimated 8.4 percent of children aged two to seventeen years (5.4 million) in the United States have a diagnosis of attention-deficit/hyperactivity disorder (ADHD). The characteristic symptoms of ADHD are inattention, hyperactivity, and impulsiveness. The *DSM-5* categorizes the disorder into three subtypes, each defined by its predominant presenting symptom: (1) ADHD, predominantly inattentive presentation; (2) ADHD, predominantly hyperactive/impulsive presentation; and (3) ADHD, combined presentation. Most children diagnosed with ADHD have the combined type. Boys are twice as likely to be diagnosed with ADHD as girls.[6]

WHAT TO WATCH FOR

Signs of Inattention
- Has Trouble Staying Focused
- Appears Not to Listen
- Has Difficulty Organizing Tasks
- Often Loses Things
- Is Easily Distracted

Signs of Hyperactivity/Impulsiveness
- Fidgets (e.g., Taps Feet)
- Has Difficulty Staying Seated
- Talks Excessively
- Struggles to Wait for a Turn
- Interrupts or Intrudes on Others

EVAN is a nine-year-old boy whose parents report his experiencing significant academic and behavioral problems. They describe him as easily frustrated and impulsive. At home he has difficulty following instructions and keeping to schedules, and he often loses things. His teacher has told his parents that he is restless and fidgety, has problems staying on task, and frequently interrupts other students. Evan recognizes that he is struggling but says that he "can't control his behavior," even though he has tried to do so. He enjoys spending time with friends and playing video games and baseball. His pediatrician has suggested that he be assessed by an educational psychologist. Evan meets *DSM-5* criteria for ADHD, combined presentation.

Anxiety Disorders. An estimated 7.1 percent of children aged three to seventeen years (4.4 million) in the United States have been diagnosed with an anxiety disorder. Common anxiety disorders among children include specific phobias, social anxiety disorder, generalized anxiety disorder, and separation anxiety disorder. The characteristic symptoms of these disorders are persistent irrational fear and panic attacks. In childhood, anxiety disorders occur equally in boys and girls, but after puberty, girls are twice as likely to be diagnosed as boys.[7]

WHAT TO WATCH FOR

- Unfounded or Unrealistic Fears
- Physical Symptoms (e.g., Headaches, Abdominal Complaints, Muscle Tension, Restlessness, and Difficulty Sleeping)
- Trouble Separating from Parents
- Nervousness or a Propensity to Be "On Edge"
- Irritability

ZOE is a twelve-year-old girl experiencing significant anxiety and problems sleeping. Her parents describe her as shy, respectful, and a "straight-A student." She has been complaining over the last six months of severe abdominal pain in the morning. The pain is never present at night. She has missed more than twenty days of school because of the pain. She has also been avoiding school field trips and her dance class, fearing she may be involved in a fatal car accident. Her parents report that she has difficulty sleeping due to worry and that, to ease her fear, she often asks her parents to lay with her in bed until she falls asleep. Zoe meets *DSM-5* criteria for generalized anxiety disorder.

Depression. Research finds that in the United States, approximately 1 percent of preschoolers one to four years old (200,000), 2 percent of school-aged children five to twelve years old (600,000), and 8 percent of adolescents thirteen to seventeen years old (2.1 million) struggle with depression. The characteristic symptom of depression is a persistently sad and empty mood. In children and adolescents, the mood can appear more as irritability than as sadness. In childhood, depression occurs equally in boys and girls, but in adolescence, girls are twice as likely to be diagnosed as boys.[8]

WHAT TO WATCH FOR

- Persistent Feelings of Sadness and Hopelessness
- Changes in Appetite (Increased or Decreased)
- Changes in Sleep Habits (Excessive Sleeping or Insomnia)
- Physical Complaints (e.g., Stomachaches, Headaches) That Do Not Respond to Treatment
- Difficulty Thinking or Concentrating
- Thoughts of Death or Suicide

CARMEN is a fifteen-year-old girl who reports sadness, frequent crying spells, decreased appetite, and difficulty concentrating. These issues were initially triggered by the breakup of a romantic relationship but have now persisted for more than three months. Her parents report that Carmen, normally a very active and social teen, now spends most of her time alone in her room sleeping. She is failing several classes and often says, "I wish I were dead" when she becomes frustrated. Her pediatrician has suggested treatment with the antidepressant Zoloft, but her parents are resistant to her taking psychiatric medication. Carmen meets *DSM-5* criteria for major depressive disorder.

Disruptive Behavior Disorders. The *DSM-5* describes two disruptive behavior disorders: oppositional defiant disorder (ODD) and conduct disorder (CD). An estimated 3 percent of children aged three to seventeen years (1.6 million) in the United States struggle with ODD or CD. Disruptive behavior disorders are characterized by problems in emotional and behavioral regulation. Symptoms include defiance of authority figures, anger outbursts, and antisocial behaviors, such as lying and stealing. Boys are twice as likely as girls to be diagnosed with ODD or CD.[9]

WHAT TO WATCH FOR

- Frequent Anger Outbursts
- Defiance or Refusal to Comply with Rules
- Antisocial Behaviors (e.g., Lying, Stealing, Bullying)
- A Lack of Empathy or Remorse
- Chronic Irritability

LANCE is a six-year-old boy whose parents are concerned about his extreme temper tantrums. His teacher reports that Lance becomes easily enraged and confrontational, refusing to follow rules or take direction. When frustrated, he becomes aggressive and destructive, breaking toys and throwing objects. Recently, Lance struck a fellow student in the head with a toy at school after the other boy asked him to share. His parents report similar problem behavior at home, particularly at bedtime and when he is getting dressed in the morning. Most disturbing is the fact that Lance appears to deliberately ignore instruction from adults and maliciously taunts his siblings and classmates. Lance meets *DSM-5* criteria for oppositional defiant disorder.

Autism Spectrum Disorder. The Centers for Disease Control and Prevention estimate that, in the United States, one in fifty-four children aged three to seventeen years (1.5 million) has autism spectrum disorder (ASD). Autism is characterized by difficulties with social interaction and communication and a tendency to engage in restricted, repetitive patterns of behavior. The *DSM-5* classifies ASD as a neurodevelopmental disorder. Neurodevelopmental disorders are conditions in which the development of the central nervous system is disrupted. Autism is four times more common in boys (one in thirty-four) than in girls (one in every one hundred forty-four).[10]

WHAT TO WATCH FOR

- Avoidance of Eye Contact
- Delayed Language Development
- Inappropriate Social Interactions
- A Preference for Solitude or Isolation
- A Propensity to Become Upset by Minor Changes in Routine
- Restricted Interests
- Persistent Repetitive Behavior (e.g., Rocking)

MICHAEL is a four-year-old boy whose parents are concerned about his delayed language development and odd repetitive movements. His expressive language consists of little more than grunts and repetitive sounds or single words when requesting attention or a desired item. Michael's mother reports that in social situations, he physically turns away from others or looks down to break eye contact. Any change to his regular routine or any new situation causes him significant distress. In addition, he displays what appear to be compulsive, repetitive movements, which include a regular yawn-like opening of his mouth and rhythmic rocking. Michael meets *DSM-5* criteria for autism spectrum disorder.

ASSESSMENT QUESTIONS

In your role as a pastoral counselor, you are likely to be contacted by concerned parents whose children are struggling with emotional and behavioral problems. When helping parents determine whether their child needs to see a professional mental health-care provider, use two tenets to guide your evaluation. First, keep in mind that when it comes to emotional and behavioral development in children, "normal" is a big tent. Children develop and mature at significantly different rates, and even the development of siblings within a family can vary dramatically. Second, remember that children are not simply little adults. As such, many behaviors that we consider symptoms of mental illness in adults, such as impulsiveness or extreme shyness, can occur as a normal part of a child's development. Therefore, it is important not to impose adult emotional and behavioral standards on them.

The following sections contain assessment questions to help you and the parents determine whether a professional referral may be necessary. The questions are similar to those in the previous chapter but are geared toward children. Follow the same process recommended for screening adults: use the format given below but ask additional questions, as needed, for clarification and follow topical trajectories in the conversation when you feel it is appropriate.

Parents' Primary Concern. First, determine the primary concern, which is the parents' description of the child's behavior that has brought them to pastoral counseling. Then use the following questions to prompt the parents to elaborate on their concern.

1. When did this problem/concern begin?
2. How has the problem progressed? For example, have there been times when the issue became better or worse?
3. Does the problem interfere with your child's ability to go to school, be involved in activities outside the home, or maintain healthy relationships?

Impairment in at least one area of daily function is often symptomatic of a mental health problem.

Child's Mental Health History. A brief history of past mental health problems and interventions the child has experienced can provide insight into the present concern. The following questions will help you gather information on the child's previous interactions with the mental health-care system. The recurrence of a mental health problem that required professional care in the past suggests that a referral may be in order.

1. Has [child's name] ever had the same or a similar problem/ concern in the past? If yes, what did you do to resolve it?
2. Has [child's name] ever seen a counselor or other mental health-care professional? If yes, for what?
3. Has [child's name] ever taken medication for a mental health problem? If yes, which medication(s)?
4. Has [child's name] ever been hospitalized for a mental health problem? If yes, how long ago?

Level of Psychological Distress. A significantly high level of psychological distress in children and adolescents indicates the presence of a mental health problem. A simple yet accurate measure of childhood psychological distress that you can easily administer in an interview format is the eight-item Brief Screening Measure of Emotional Distress (BSMED).[11] Answers to the questions are based on the parents' account of their child's functioning during the past week. Each item is scored from 0 to 2 using the following scale: does not apply (0 points), applies somewhat (1 point), or certainly applies (2 points).

Please answer each question based on [child's name]'s level of functioning during the past week.
1. Did [child's name] appear **worried about many things?**
2. Did [child's name] appear **miserable, unhappy, tearful, or depressed?**
3. Did [child's name] **show little enjoyment in things?**
4. Did [child's name] **have tears about doing some things?**
5. Has [child's name] been **irritable or quarrelsome?**
6. Has [child's name] been **complaining of aches and pains?**
7. Has [child's name] been **withdrawn and quiet?**
8. Did [child's name] appear **forgetful or show poor concentration?**

Once the parents have answered all the questions, add the points to obtain a total score. Total scores on the BSMED can range from 0 to 16 and are interpreted as follows: 0–2 = no psychological distress, 3–5 = mild psychological distress, 6–8 = moderate psychological distress, and 9–16 = severe psychological distress. Children displaying severe psychological distress are likely to meet *DSM-5* criteria for a mental disorder and should be referred to a licensed mental health-care provider.

Attention and Behavioral Control. ADHD is one of the most common mental disorders affecting children and teens. The following questions will help you gather information on the child's ability to focus his attention and regulate his behavior. Using the following scale, parents score each statement from 0 to 2 based on how accurately it relates to their child: never true (0 points), sometimes true (1 point), or often true (2 points).

1. My child is distractible and has trouble sticking to a task.
2. My child fails to finish things he/she starts.
3. My child has difficulty following directions or instructions.
4. My child is impulsive and acts without stopping to think.
5. My child jumps from one activity to another.
6. My child fidgets.

Once the parents have responded to all the statements, add up the points to obtain a total score. A score of 7 points or higher suggests problems with inattention and impulsiveness.[12]

Presence of Oppositional Behavior. The questions in this section will help you differentiate between normal childhood disobedience and the presence of a disruptive behavior disorder. Using the following scale, parents score each statement from 0 to 2 based on how accurately it relates to their child: never true (0 points), sometimes true (1 point), or often true (2 points).

1. My child is cranky.
2. My child is defiant and talks back to adults.
3. My child blames others for his/her own mistakes.
4. My child is easily annoyed by others.
5. My child argues a lot with adults.
6. My child is angry and resentful.

Once the parents have responded to all the statements, add up the points to obtain a total score. A score of 7 points or higher suggests a persistent problem with defiant and hostile behavior.[13]

Presence of Antisocial Behavior. The items in this section relate to violating rules and aggressive behavior. Using the following scale, parents score each statement from 0 to 2 based on how accurately it relates to their child: never true (0 points), sometimes true (1 point), or often true (2 points).

1. My child breaks rules at home.
2. My child breaks rules at school.
3. My child gets into fights.
4. My child skips school.
5. My child runs away from home.
6. My child gets into trouble for lying or stealing.

Once the parents have responded to all the statements, add the points to obtain a total score. A score of 3 points or higher suggests a problematic pattern of antisocial behavior.[14]

Risk of Suicidality and Self-Harm. A child or adolescent is at a heightened risk of suicide if they have a history of self-harm or suicide attempts, especially if they are showing moderate to severe levels of psychological distress. Suicide risk is further increased if the child is actively abusing alcohol or drugs.

1. Has [child's name] ever attempted suicide? If yes, when?
2. Are you presently concerned that [child's name] is thinking about killing himself/herself?
3. Has [child's name] been talking about death or dying?
4. Has [child's name] wished they were dead or that they could go to sleep and never wake up?
5. Has [child's name] intentionally harmed himself/herself recently (e.g., cutting, burning)?

6. Do you believe that [child's name] is presently using alcohol or drugs?

An answer of yes to any of these questions suggests that the child or adolescent is actively struggling with a mental health problem. Immediate help from emergency personnel should be sought for any child that is currently having suicidal thoughts.

CASE EXAMPLE

The following case example shows how you might use the question sets above to assess the mental health needs of a child.

NELSON and Jean have been married for ten years and have two children, eight-year-old Jack and seven-month-old John. Nelson is a self-employed plumber and Jean is a homemaker. They have been members of the church for the last five years. The couple is actively involved in a small group Bible study and regularly attends the Sunday morning service. Before this year, Jean had homeschooled Jack, but the couple decided to send him to public school for third grade, after the birth of John. Jack has been having trouble both academically and behaviorally at school, and the couple has come for counsel because his teacher recommended that he be assessed by a child and adolescent psychologist for ADHD.

Parents' Primary Concern

I'd like to ask you a series of questions that will help me better understand Jack's present struggles and help us find the best course of action. When did this problem/concern with Jack begin?
▶ "Jack's teacher scheduled a meeting with us last week. She said that he is having trouble keeping up academically. He also gets in trouble almost every day for talking or being out of his seat. We just don't understand what is going on. He is so well behaved at home."

How has the problem progressed? For example, have there been times when the issue became better or worse?

▶ "Everything seemed fine for the first few months of school, but then we noticed that he was not getting his star every day. On his last report card, he received an Unsatisfactory for conduct. We talked to him about his behavior at school and punished him for being disobedient. He also brings work home almost every day that he isn't able to finish in class. I asked some of the other mothers about their children, and they all seem to be able to finish their work at school."

Does the problem interfere with Jack's ability to go to school, be involved in activities outside the home, or maintain healthy relationships?

▶ "Jack has always loved school, but now he cries in the morning and doesn't want to go. We feel that the teacher has labeled him as the 'bad kid' and treats him differently. I don't understand. When I was home-schooling him, he had no problem with the lessons and was always well behaved. Do you think I should start homeschooling him again?"

Child's Mental Health History

Has Jack ever had the same or a similar problem/concern in the past?
▶ "No."

Has Jack ever seen a counselor or other mental health-care professional?
▶ "No."

Has Jack ever taken medication for a mental health problem?
▶ "No, and that is what we are concerned about. They just want to put him on medication to control him. We are afraid it will change him into a different little boy."

Level of Psychological Distress

I'm going to ask you some questions, and I'd like you to answer them based on Jack's level of functioning during the past week:

*Did Jack appear **worried about many things?** Would you say this statement does not apply (0), applies somewhat (1), or certainly applies (2)?*
❱ "Applies somewhat." [1 point]

*Did Jack appear **miserable, unhappy, tearful, or depressed?** Does not apply (0), applies somewhat (1), or certainly applies (2)?*
❱ "Does not apply." [0 points]

*Did Jack show **little enjoyment in things?** Does not apply (0), applies somewhat (1), or certainly applies (2)?*
❱ "Does not apply." [0 points]

*Did Jack have **tears about doing some things?** Does not apply (0), applies somewhat (1), or certainly applies (2)?*
❱ "Certainly applies. He cries every morning before we go to school." [2 points]

*Has Jack been **irritable and quarrelsome?** Does not apply (0), applies somewhat (1), or certainly applies (2)?*
❱ "Applies somewhat." [1 point]

*Has Jack been **complaining of aches and pains?** Does not apply (0), applies somewhat (1), or certainly applies (2)?*
❱ "Certainly applies. Almost every morning he says his stomach hurts or he's going to throw up and doesn't want to go to school." [2 points]

*Has Jack been **withdrawn and quiet?** Does not apply (0), applies somewhat (1), or certainly applies (2)?*
❱ "Does not apply." [0 points]

*Did Jack appear **forgetful and show poor concentration?** Does not apply (0), applies somewhat (1), or certainly applies (2)?*
❱ "Applies somewhat. Jack has always been forgetful." [1 point]

Attention and Behavioral Control

Tell me how accurately you feel each of these statements relates to Jack:

My child is distractible and has trouble sticking to a task. Would you say this is never true (0), sometimes true (1), or often true (2)?

▶ "Sometimes true." [1 point]

My child fails to finish things he starts. Never true (0), sometimes true (1), or often true (2)?

▶ "Often true." [2 points]

My child has difficulty following directions or instructions. Never true (0), sometimes true (1), or often true (2)?

▶ "His teacher says that he doesn't listen to her, but he is very obedient at home. So I guess sometimes true." [1 point]

My child is impulsive and acts without stopping to think. Never true (0), sometimes true (1), or often true (2)?

▶ "Isn't that normal for all little boys? Sometimes true." [1 point]

My child jumps from one activity to another. Never true (0), sometimes true (1), or often true (2)?

▶ "Never true." [0 points]

My child fidgets. Never true (0), sometimes true (1), or often true (2)?

▶ "Jack has always been full of energy. Often true." [2 points]

Presence of Oppositional Behavior

Now, tell me how accurately you feel each of these statements relates to Jack:

My child is cranky. Never true (0), sometimes true (1), or often true (2)?

▶ "Sometimes true. He has only been that way since these problems at school have started." [1 point]

My child is defiant and talks back to adults. Never true (0), sometimes true (1), or often true (2)?

▶ "Never true." [0 points]

My child blames others for his own mistakes. Never true (0), sometimes true (1), or often true (2)?
▶ "Never true." [0 points]

My child is easily annoyed by others. Never true (0), sometimes true (1), or often true (2)?
▶ "Never true." [0 points]

My child argues a lot with adults. Never true (0), sometimes true (1), or often true (2)?
▶ "Never true." [0 points]

My child is angry and resentful. Never true (0), sometimes true (1), or often true (2)?
▶ "Never true." [0 points]

Presence of Antisocial Behavior

Next, rate these statements as they relate to Jack:

My child breaks rules at home. Never true (0), sometimes true (1), or often true (2)?
▶ "Never true." [0 points]

My child breaks rules at school. Never true (0), sometimes true (1), or often true (2)?
▶ "Sometimes true." [1 point]

My child gets into fights. Never true (0), sometimes true (1), or often true (2)?
▶ "Never true." [0 points]

My child skips school. Never true (0), sometimes true (1), or often true (2)?
▶ "Never true." [0 points]

My child runs away from home. Never true (0), sometimes true (1), or often true (2)?
▶ "Never true." [0 points]

My child gets into trouble for lying or stealing. Never true (0), sometimes true (1), or often true (2)?
❯ "Never true." [0 points]

Risk of Suicidality and Self-Harm

Finally, has Jack been talking about death or dying?
❯ "No."

Has Jack wished he were dead or that he could go to sleep and never wake up?
❯ "No."

Has Jack intentionally harmed himself recently (e.g., cutting, burning)?
❯ "No."

Do you believe that Jack is presently using alcohol or drugs?
❯ "No."

JACK'S MENTAL HEALTH RED FLAGS

- He is having academic difficulties.
- He displays behavioral problems at school.
- He shows clinically significant levels of inattention and impulsiveness.
- He is experiencing moderate psychological distress (with a BSMED score of 7).

Nelson and Jean's responses to the interview questions suggest that Jack's mental health issues may be the cause of his academic and behavioral difficulties at school. A referral to a child and adolescent psychologist for a psychological assessment is strongly suggested.

Unfortunately, many parents are resistant to the idea of their child seeing a psychologist or psychiatrist. They often hope that changes in diet, discipline, or spiritual engagement will take care of their child's problems. As a pastoral counselor, you have the opportunity to ease any concerns they have about mental health care and to break the stigma surrounding it. You also have the chance to encourage their desire to see their child healthy and whole. Often, good first steps in this direction are to help them understand that God has created their child as a physical, mental, spiritual, and relational being, and to help them realize that mental health-care providers and treatments are part of God's providential grace toward us.

PROMOTING PSYCHOLOGICAL WELL-BEING

As a pastoral counselor, you likely will be asked by parents how they can protect their children from developing mental health problems. Mental disorders result from a complex interaction of biological vulnerabilities and environmental stressors. While there is little that can be done about a child's biology, parents can certainly alter the level of stress to which their child is exposed. The following are simple suggestions for how parents can reduce damaging stress and increase a child's psychological well-being.

Create Structure and Routine. Routines and schedules reduce stress and anxiety. They allow a child to take a break from making decisions or guessing about the future. A daily structure and routine gives a child a sense of safety and predictability.

Teach Resiliency. An important factor in psychological well-being is resiliency, or how well a person can cope with and bounce back from stress and adversity (e.g., bullying, academic difficulties, and social rejection). Resiliency is not something one is born with. Rather, it is something that is learned and modeled. Parents can help children develop resiliency by teaching them to solve problems independently and by modeling positive approaches to coping when they encounter challenges in their own lives.

Reduce Parental Distress and Conflict. A child does not have the experience, emotional maturity, or cognitive skills necessary to deal with adult problems. Financial issues, legal problems, and marital discord are simply too overwhelming for a child. Parents should work out their personal distress and conflicts privately, away from their children.

Make Home a Safe Haven. Parents should make their home and family a safe haven. A safe haven is a place where a child knows he is loved and accepted for who he is, not for how he performs. It is also a place where parents are actively engaged in their child's daily life and intentional about providing opportunities for him to ask questions and share concerns.

Advocate for Children with Academic Issues. Academic achievement is often equated with success. However, children vary significantly in how they learn. Some children find school easy and rewarding, while others struggle to keep up with their peers. A child should see her parent as an advocate and cheerleader in her education, not as a task master. Parents should get to know their child's teacher so that they fully understand her academic strengths and weaknesses. Together, parents and teachers should set realistic academic goals based on the child's abilities. If a child struggles, take advantage of after-school programs and tutors. A child's mental health is far more important than her grades.

Make Spiritual Life a Priority. Children who are able to connect with an entity larger than themselves are able to cope better with stress, resulting in lower blood pressure and stress hormone levels. They also report less anxiety, less depression, and increased feelings of security, compassion, and love. Parents should make faith a priority within the family.

BEING INCLUSIVE

A child living with mental health problems has the same spiritual needs as any other child: to hear the gospel, to grow in Christ, and to be part of a supportive and loving fellowship of believers. Churches must be prepared for families struggling with childhood mental health problems before these families arrive at the door. These three simple steps will help any size of church to ensure it has an inclusive child and youth ministry:

1. Ensure all staff and volunteers working with children and youth at the church receive training in how to recognize and respond to the signs and symptoms of mental illness in youth.
2. Develop a buddy system within the children's ministry. In a buddy system, older students in the youth group, college

Children Are a Gift

God is intimately involved in the creation of every new life. All children, including those with mental health problems, are "fearfully and wonderfully made" in his image. For parents struggling to care for a child with a mental disorder, the church should be a place of grace and unconditional love rather than a place of ignorance and shame.

SUGGESTED SCRIPTURES

Psalm 127:3   Children are a blessing and a gift from God.

Jeremiah 1:5   God knows and desires a relationship with each child.

Matthew 19:13–15   Jesus has a heart for children.

BIBLICAL STORY TO CONNECT

The Syrophoenician Woman's Daughter

Matthew 15:21–28   Do not allow stigma or circumstances to keep you from finding healing for your child.

ministry, or general church congregation are recruited to serve as buddies, offering necessary one-on-one support during Sunday school time to children living with a mental health problem. A buddy system allows all children to participate in the church's mainstream programs, which is a more inclusive approach than relocating everyone with special needs to a separate classroom or expecting the family to offer support to the child.

3. Encourage children- and youth-ministry leaders to adopt a partnership approach to ministry, joining with parents of children who suffer with mental illness. This should involve an initial meeting with parents, where leaders ask, "What are your child's special needs?" and "How can we engage and support your child?" Parents can then share tips, tactics, and strategies that have worked at home and in school, which can be incorporated into the child's Sunday morning classroom experience. Thereafter, updates and feedback opportunities between the parents and ministry leaders should be ongoing and occur regularly.

A faith community should be a safe haven for children struggling with mental health problems and their parents. Jesus is calling all children to himself (Luke 18:15–17), and we must not let church tradition or ceremony keep those with mental illness away. When God places a struggling family in our path, we have the opportunity to demonstrate the compassion and grace of the Savior who sacrificed all so that we might know him.

Referral

Suicidal Thoughts and Behavior

Faith communities are unfortunately not immune to the tragedy of suicide. In a recent LifeWay Research survey focusing on suicide and the church, almost a third (27 percent) of Protestant pastors reported a suicide connected with their church in the last year. In the same survey, 32 percent of Protestant churchgoers reported a close family member or acquaintance had taken their own lives.[1] While pastoral counselors have an obvious part to play in the care of survivors, they also serve an important preventative role in relation to suicide.

Lilly has struggled with a psychotic disorder since her late teens that causes her to hear voices and, at times, become paranoid and delusional to the point of being hospitalized. Recently she fell behind in her classes, due to a decline in her mental health, so she left college and moved in with her grandmother Betty. She hoped that living with her grandmother would give her an opportunity to get healthy and return to college the following year. Then one Saturday morning, her grandmother awoke to find Lilly in a highly agitated and emotional state. She was pacing around her room, unable to be still, talking to the voices. On this day, the voices were ordering her to kill herself, and she was struggling not to follow their commands. Fearing for her granddaughter's life, Betty called Justin, a pastoral counselor who had met with Lilly several times in the past.

Justin came to the house and spoke with Lilly for several minutes. After recognizing that she was suicidal, he suggested that they go to the emergency room at a nearby hospital. Lilly was very resistant to his suggestion because she feared that she may be hospitalized again. After some discussion, Justin agreed to stay with Lilly as she tried to work through the episode. For the remainder of the morning and into the afternoon, Justin talked with Lilly about her identity in Christ, the character of God, and God's presence in times of human suffering. Lilly would frantically pace around her bedroom, talking and laughing. At other times, she would curl up in a fetal position in her bed and weep. Justin was a reassuring and calming presence to Lilly throughout the day. As the hours passed, Lilly became less and less agitated and more in control of her emotions. The voices began to disappear into the background. By late afternoon, the voices had stopped commanding Lilly to harm herself, and she was no longer considering suicide. Convinced that she was now safe, Justin left Lilly under the watchful eye of Betty and called the next morning to check on her. Lilly continued to be fine throughout the remainder of the weekend and met with her psychiatrist on Monday morning.

STATISTICS AND TRENDS

Suicide rates in the United States are on the rise, having increased more than 30 percent over the first two decades of this century.[2] In 2018, over 48,000 people took their own lives. To put that number in perspective, there are more than twice as many suicides in the United States every year as there are homicides. On average, 129 people die by suicide every day. Suicide is the tenth leading cause of death overall in the United States and the second leading cause of death among those ten to thirty-four years old.[3] While suicide can happen at any age, the highest suicide rate is found in those forty-five to fifty-four years of age. The second highest rate occurs in those eighty-five years or older.[4]

The phenomenon of suicide, however, is far more complex than the number of people who die. In 2018, 10.7 million Americans (eighteen and over) reported that they had serious thoughts of killing themselves. Of those, 3.3 million made a suicide plan and 1.4 million made a nonfatal suicide attempt.[5] In fact, it is estimated that there is only one death for every twenty-five suicide attempts made. Women are more likely than men to have suicidal thoughts and twice as likely to make a suicide attempt. Men, on the other hand, die by suicide at nearly four times the rate of women, accounting for 75 percent of all suicide deaths. This gender difference in fatalities is due to the fact that men tend to use more lethal means when attempting suicide (i.e., firearms and hanging) and are less likely to receive mental health treatment than women. In the United States, firearms are the most common method used in suicide, accounting for just over half of all deaths.[6]

RISK FACTORS

A history of mental illness significantly increases an individual's risk for suicide. Research has found that 90 percent of those who die by suicide meet criteria for a mental disorder at the time of their death.[7] Disorders with markedly increased rates of suicide include borderline personality disorder, major depressive disorder, bipolar disorder, schizophrenia, eating disorders, and substance use disorders.[8] Environmental factors such as stressful life events (e.g., social rejection, divorce, the death of a loved one, financial crisis), exposure to another person's suicide, and prolonged stressful circumstances (e.g., harassment, bullying, abuse, unemployment, serious illness, chronic pain) all increase a person's risk. Previous suicide attempts, a family history of suicide, and easy access to lethal means have been shown to increase suicide risk as well.

COMMON MYTHS

A large percentage of the general population hold inaccurate beliefs about suicide. These suicide myths hinder people from accessing proper mental health care and limit prevention efforts. The church must actively work to dispel these myths if we are going to effectively minister to the psychologically distressed individuals that God is sending to us.

MYTH: *People who talk about taking their own lives are only trying to get attention or manipulate others. They won't really do it.*

FACT: Talk of taking one's life is a sign of severe psychological distress and requires immediate action. Research shows that approximately one-third of individuals who have suicidal thoughts will progress to making a suicide plan, and one-third of those individuals will make a suicide attempt within their lifetime.[9] Sixty percent of individuals who transition from thinking about suicide to making an attempt do so within one year after the onset of suicidal thoughts.[10]

MYTH: *Asking people if they are thinking about or considering suicide will lead to or encourage suicidal behavior.*

FACT: Research finds that talking openly about suicide actually reduces suicidal thoughts and leads to overall improvement in the mental health of those seeking treatment.[11]

MYTH: *Most suicides happen suddenly and without warning.*

FACT: Warning signs precede most suicides. Research suggests that the majority of people who attempt suicide communicate directly or indirectly about their suicidal thoughts and intent to kill themselves prior to their attempt.[12]

MYTH: *Psychiatric hospitalization reduces an individual's suicide risk.*

FACT: While inpatient psychiatric hospitalization is often necessary for individuals in imminent danger of taking their own lives, hospitalization itself does not actually reduce a person's risk for suicide. Research shows that suicide risk is actually highest in the weeks immediately following discharge from the hospital.[13] Continued vigilance following discharge, by pastoral counselors and family members, is necessary to keep those at risk safe.

MYTH: *Once someone is suicidal, he will always remain suicidal.*

FACT: Suicidal intent changes over time. The majority of individuals who have suicidal thoughts will never attempt to take their own lives. Increased suicide risk is often short term and situation-specific. For example, in a study of over five hundred individuals restrained from jumping off the Golden Gate Bridge, 94 percent were still alive twenty-six years later.[14]

ASSESSING SUICIDAL RISK

Expressing ideas of suicide or a desire to die is the single strongest indicator of increased suicidal risk. This may present as overtly threatening to hurt or kill oneself, talking about wanting to die, actively seeking means to kill oneself, or posting on social media about death and suicide. Less obvious warning signs include communicating feelings of hopelessness, having no purpose, being trapped, being in unbearable pain, and being a burden to others. If you are concerned that a counselee may be a danger to herself, use the following questions to assess her level of risk.

1. Do you feel hopeless about the present or future?
2. Have you ever intentionally harmed yourself or attempted suicide?
3. Are you having thoughts about taking your life? (If yes, move on to question 4.)
4. Do you currently have a plan to take your life? (If yes, move on to question 5.)
5. Do you have the means necessary to carry out your plan?

An individual is at a heightened risk of suicide if she has a history of self-harm or suicide attempts, especially if she also expressed hopelessness. Suicide risk is further increased if the person is actively abusing alcohol or drugs. Immediate help from emergency personnel should be sought for any counselee who has suicidal thoughts or a plan. This can be done by taking the suicidal individual to a hospital emergency room or by calling 911 and explaining the nature of the mental health emergency. A third option would be to call the National Suicide Prevention Lifeline at 800-273-TALK (8255) and have the person speak with a trained suicide counselor.

CASE EXAMPLE

If possible, the risk-assessment questions above should be used as part of the broader mental health assessment described in chapter 3 (for an adult) or chapter 4 (for a youth). The following case example shows how you might use these new questions as part of the larger interview process to assess a person's suicidal risk.

SUSAN is a thirty-eight-year-old recently divorced mother of two. She and her ex-husband, Ron, previously met with their pastor for marital counseling, until eight months ago, when Ron began an extramarital affair, separated from Susan, and filed for divorce. The church has been assisting Susan and her children financially since the separation. Before the separation, the family was actively involved at the church, but Susan and her children have not attended in the past four months. She is seeking pastoral counseling, wondering how to move forward with her life.

Primary Complaint or Concern

Susan, I'd like to ask you a series of questions to help me better understand your present struggles and help us find the best course of action. Tell me how you've been.

❱ "Frankly, I feel numb. It's been a rough year for me and the kids. I'm having stress-related headaches, increasing anxiety, fatigue, and pain in my stomach. Ron just discarded us and moved on with his new life. I feel like I've failed as a wife and a mother."

How have these mood and physical problems progressed over the last few months? Have there been times they became better or worse?
❱ "I've struggled since Ron left, but they have definitely increased in severity since I received the final divorce papers about a month ago."

Has this interfered with your ability to work or maintain healthy relationships?
❱ "It's been hard to care for the boys. My mom comes over several times a week to help out. Most days, it's all I can do to get out of bed. I know I've pushed everyone away, but it's just easier to be home alone. I've been applying for jobs, but I'm not even sure I'll be able to work. Honestly, most of the time, life is not worth living."

Mental Health History

Have you ever had the same or similar feelings in the past?
❱ "No."

Have you ever seen a counselor or other mental health-care professional?
❱ "Only you, for marital counseling."

Have you ever taken medication for a mental health problem?
❱ "I saw my primary care physician for my abdominal pain. While I was there, she prescribed an antidepressant for me. I've been taking it for about a month. I don't think it is helping."

Use of Alcohol and Drugs

Do you enjoy a drink now and then? If yes, how often?
❱ "I occasionally have a glass of wine, but it's been awhile."

Have you used drugs, including prescription drugs, in the past year?
▶ "No."

Have these thoughts and feelings caused you to drink more often than usual?
▶ "No."

Level of Psychological Distress

I'm going to ask you some questions, and I'd like you to answer them based on how you have felt over the last thirty days.

*How often during the past thirty days did you feel **nervous?** Would you say all of the time (4), most of the time (3), some of the time (2), a little of the time (1), or none of the time?*
▶ "All of the time." [4 points]

*During the past thirty days, how often did you feel **hopeless?** All of the time (4), most of the time (3), some of the time (2), a little of the time (1), or none of the time (0)?*
▶ "All of the time." [4 points]

*During the past thirty days, how often did you feel **restless or fidgety?** All of the time (4), most of the time (3), some of the time (2), a little of the time (1), or none of the time (0)?*
▶ "Some of the time." [2 points]

*During the past thirty days, how often did you feel **so depressed that nothing could cheer you up?** All of the time (4), most of the time (3), some of the time (2), a little of the time (1), or none of the time (0)?*
▶ "Most of the time." [3 points]

*During the past thirty days, how often did you feel **that everything was an effort?** All of the time (4), most of the time (3), some of the time (2), a little of the time (1), or none of the time (0)?*
▶ "All of the time." [4 points]

*During the past thirty days, how often did you feel **worthless**? All of the time (4), most of the time (3), some of the time (2), a little of the time (1), or none of the time (0)?*
▶ "All of the time." [4 points]

Suicidality

Do you feel hopeless about the present or future?
▶ "Completely. I'm not sure there is a future for me."

Have you ever intentionally harmed yourself or attempted suicide?
▶ "No."

Are you having thoughts about taking your life?
▶ "Yes. I have had those thoughts over the last month. Sometimes I think it might just be better for everyone if I was gone."

Do you currently have a plan to take your life?
▶ "I'm embarrassed to say that I have stashed some pills away in case I ever get up enough nerve to do it. I know it would be wrong, but I don't think I can continue to live like this."

SUSAN'S MENTAL HEALTH RED FLAGS

- She has had a persistent, progressive decline in mood.
- There has been a negative impact on her relationships and home life.
- She is experiencing severe psychological distress (with a K6 score of 21).
- She is having suicidal thoughts.
- She has a suicide plan and access to lethal means.

Susan's responses to the assessment questions show that she is at significant risk of harming herself. Susan's heightened suicidality requires an immediate response. She should be taken to an emergency room or mental health crisis clinic for further psychiatric evaluation. If she refuses, you should call 911.

IS SUICIDE A SIN?

The Bible lists seven men who took their own lives: Abimelech (Judg. 9:52–54), Samson (Judg. 16:23–31), King Saul and his armor bearer (1 Sam. 31:1–5), Ahithophel (2 Sam. 17:23), Zimri (1 Kings 16:18), and Judas Iscariot (Matt. 27:3–5). In addition, some of the most revered heroes of the faith, including Job, Elijah, and King David, struggled with suicidal thoughts. Since its beginning, the church has struggled with understanding the spiritual consequences of suicide, at times even refusing religious rites to the victims who were thought to have committed an unforgivable sin, damning them to hell.

While Christian tradition has historically considered suicide a sin, there is no direct prohibition against suicide in either the Old or New Testament. Saint Augustine (354–430 AD), perhaps the most influential church father in western Christianity, considered suicide self-murder and a violation of the sixth commandment, "You shall not murder" (Ex. 20:13; Deut. 5:17). Thomas Aquinas (1225–1274 AD), the thirteenth-century theologian and philosopher, continued this line of thinking by arguing that suicide was a sin because life is God's gift to man and only God has the right to take it away. He based his thoughts on Deuteronomy 32:39, "It is I who put to death and give life."

While these are both sensible interpretations of scripture in relation to suicide, there is one significant caveat that must be mentioned. Augustine and Aquinas both considered suicide to be a reasoned decision. They believed that the suicidal individual was making a rational choice to violate God's will for his life. Their thinking was, at least in part, based on a faulty understanding of suicidal motivations. Understandably, they had no appreciation for the role that mental illness plays in suicide.

Today, although many Catholic, Orthodox, and Protestant clergy still consider the act of suicide a sin, the church is generally compassionate toward those who take their own life because they are aware of the role that mental illness or severe emotional distress plays in suicide. Suicide is now recognized as neither reasoned nor rational.

Suicidality and Faith

The Bible describes a number of faithful individuals who struggled with suicidal thoughts. Having faith, even strong faith, does not guarantee that, during times of extreme psychological distress, an individual will not consider suicide as a way out. The scriptures teach us that God provides comfort to those who cry out to him in their time of hopelessness.

SUGGESTED SCRIPTURES

Matthew 26:38   Jesus experienced and understands overwhelming sorrow.

John 5:24   Salvation comes by faith and is eternally secure.

1 Timothy 1:1   Jesus is our hope.

BIBLICAL STORY TO CONNECT

Job

Job 3:1–26   Job longs for death, yet God is present with him in his suffering and rewards him for his faithfulness.

PASTORAL CARE AND SUICIDE

As a pastoral counselor, you are likely to be called upon to minister to two different types of individuals in relation to suicide: (1) those who are struggling with suicidality (i.e., suicidal thoughts, gestures, or attempts) and (2) the families and friends of those who have died by suicide.

Those Struggling with Suicidality. The most important spiritual principle that you can encourage for those struggling with suicidal thoughts and behavior is hope. Hopelessness is intimately associated with suicidality. To most, hope is simply a feeling. It is wishful thinking for the future. Unfortunately, feelings are easily swayed by circumstances, and in difficult times, we can lose hope. To the Christian, however, hope is more than a feeling. It is a confident expectation that God's good and perfect will is being worked out in our lives. The believer's hope transcends circumstances because it is strongly linked to our faith in an unchanging, loving God. The writer of Hebrews says it this way: "Now faith is confidence in what we hope for and assurance about what we do not see" (Heb. 11:1). When working with a counselee who is struggling with suicidal thoughts and behaviors, use scriptures to help them build "hope and a future" (Jeremiah 29:11).

Individuals struggling with suicidal thoughts and behaviors often also feel worthless and of little value to family, friends, and the world around them. As believers, our value and worth are not based on our performance or on what others might think of us but rather on the fact that we have been "fearfully and wonderfully" (Psalm 139:14) made in the very image and likeness of God. Circumstances and struggles do not define who we are; God does. In Christ, we were chosen before the foundation of the world (Eph. 1:4); predestined for adoption as sons and daughters of the living God (Eph. 1:5); redeemed out of slavery to sin and death (Eph. 1:7); loved completely and unconditionally (1 John 3:1); forgiven of all our past, present, and future sins (1 John 1:9); given spiritual wisdom and revelation (Eph. 1:9); and marked as such until the day we stand before him, holy and blameless (Eph. 1:13). These are the truths of Scripture that pastoral counselors must continually remind those struggling with suicidality of, so that they might recognize their true value and worth.

Surviving Families and Friends. In the aftermath of a congregant's suicide, family, friends, and fellow church members are left with a painful mixture of grief, confusion, guilt, anger, and concern for the deceased's eternal destiny. When a congregant takes his life because psychological distress has overwhelmed him, our response as pastoral counselors should be one of grace toward his legacy and one of sympathy and compassion toward his family and friends. The gospel makes no room for fear, shame, and condemnation in any instance, and as a church, we must follow suit when we lose a brother or sister to suicide. In particular, the Bible also does not condemn those who commit suicide, and in many instances, it reports that individuals who committed suicide were shown honor after their death (e.g., Ahithophel in 2 Sam. 17:23). Suicide does not appear to have been an event that would tarnish a righteous individual's legacy in biblical times, and it shouldn't in our time either.

Suicide also does not appear to disqualify an individual from eternal life with God. Samson is our best example of this principle. Although he struggled with staying true to his faith and ultimately took his own life, the Bible records him in the Hebrews 11 "roll call of faith." When an individual comes to a saving faith in Jesus, she is made righteous and forgiven for every sin (including suicide). If that individual, for whatever reason, dies by suicide, she is ushered into the presence of Christ because she is a redeemed child of God. Suicide is not the determining factor for eternal life with God; a saving faith in Jesus is.

Finally, it is important to help the family understand that when a loved one sadly follows through with his suicidal thoughts, no one is to blame. Sometimes, no matter how hard we try, those we love still act on their hopeless feelings and end their lives.

Mental Illness and Violence

I n today's news and entertainment, people with mental health conditions are often depicted as dangerous, violent, and unpredictable. The viewing public are repeatedly vicariously exposed to insane killers and violent mental patients, causing an exaggerated association between mental illness and violence. For example, a recent national survey found that 60 percent of Americans believe people with schizophrenia are likely to act violently toward someone else, while more than a third think people with major depression are potentially violent.[1]

The media, in pursuit of ratings, sensationalizes violent crimes—particularly mass shootings—often focusing on vague and unsubstantiated reports of "mental health problems" in the perpetrator's past as the primary cause. Even our political leaders have been influenced by these misleading reports. In response to reporters' questions concerning the 2017 killing rampage at First Baptist Church in Sutherland Springs, Texas, the deadliest mass shooting in a place of worship in U.S. history, President Donald J. Trump said, "I think that mental health is your problem here. This was a very, based on preliminary reports, very deranged individual with a lot of problems over a long period of time," echoing the commonly held belief that mental illness leads to violence.[2] But does psychiatric research support this belief? Are the mentally ill more likely than those without mental illness to commit acts of violence?

ASSOCIATION BETWEEN MENTAL ILLNESS AND VIOLENCE

Research using national crime data finds that only 3 to 5 percent of violent acts in the United States are attributable to people with serious mental illness, such as schizophrenia or bipolar disorder.[3] Most people with serious mental illness do not commit violent acts, and the vast majority of violent acts are not committed by people with diagnosed mental disorders. In fact, individuals living with serious mental illness are more likely to be the victims of violence than the perpetrators.[4]

The seminal study of the association between mental illness and violence, the MacArthur Violence Risk Assessment Study, found that individuals diagnosed with a serious mental illness are no more likely to engage in violent acts than their non-substance-abusing neighborhood controls. However, if a person with a serious mental illness also has a substance use disorder, their risk of violence doubles. It has been suggested that this increased risk of violence results from the fact that a mental disorder increases the behavioral disinhibition (impulsiveness) associated with substance abuse, while the use of alcohol or drugs exacerbates the impaired judgment, paranoia, misperceptions, lack of insight, and delusional thinking associated with serious mental illness. The MacArthur study also found that when individuals with serious mental illness do become violent, the most likely target is a family member or friend (87 percent), and the violence usually occurs in the home.[5]

The relationship between serious mental illness and violence is complex and is best understood through the accumulation of many risk factors. While these risk factors may include the diagnosis of a serious mental disorder, the diagnosis of a mental disorder alone is not a specific predictor of violence.

RISK FACTORS FOR VIOLENCE

A number of demographic, psychological, and economic factors have been shown to increase the risk of violence in individuals both with and without serious mental illness. These include a younger age, a single marital status, being male, a lower socioeconomic status, a history of head trauma, early exposure to violence (e.g., domestic abuse), poor behavioral control, an antisocial personality, involvement in substance abuse, lower intelligence, easy access to weapons, and a history of violent behavior. In individuals diagnosed with serious mental illness, the following factors have also been shown to increase the risk of violence: paranoid or persecutory delusions, violent command hallucinations (i.e., auditory hallucinations that instruct the person to act violently), and nonadherence to treatment recommendations.[6]

MASS SHOOTINGS AT PLACES OF WORSHIP

The modern era of mass shootings began on August 1, 1966, when Charles Whitman opened fire on unsuspecting students and faculty from atop the clock tower at the University of Texas, killing fourteen and wounding thirty-one. A mass shooting is defined as "a multiple-homicide incident in which four or more victims are murdered with firearms, not including the offender(s), within one event, and at least some of the murders occurred in a public location or locations in close geographical proximity (e.g., a workplace, school, restaurant, or other public settings), and the murders are not attributable to any other underlying criminal activity (e.g., armed robbery)."[7] Contrary to the media's portrayal and the general public's perception, mass shootings are extremely rare events, accounting for less than two-tenths of 1 percent of all homicides in the United States. While uncommon, however, these horrific events have seen a disturbing increase in frequency over the last two decades.[8]

Since it is difficult for the average person to imagine why a sane individual would deliberately kill multiple strangers, it is wrongly assumed by most that the perpetrators of all mass shootings are mentally ill. Research, however, has not been able to establish a reliable link between mass shootings and serious mental illness. Yet, despite that fact, this is often the type of violence that pastors and ministry staff are most concerned about in relation to those with mental illness.

The Violence Project, presently the most comprehensive database of mass shootings, reports eleven mass shootings at places of worship in the United States. Three occurred prior to 2000 and eight have occurred since. The final two incidences, at First Baptist Church in Sutherland Springs, Texas (in 2017, killing twenty-six and wounding twenty), and at the Tree of Life Synagogue in Pittsburgh, Pennsylvania (in 2018, killing eleven and wounding six), were the most deadly. The perpetrators of these eleven mass shootings share a set of common demographic characteristics. All were male, and most were single (64 percent), white (82 percent), in their twenties (45 percent) or forties (45 percent), and unemployed (64 percent). Most of them also had a history of substance abuse (82 percent) and violence (75 percent). Seven of the perpetrators died by suicide during the event, and the remainder were arrested. It is unclear whether serious mental illness played a role in any of these mass shootings.[9]

It is easiest, and perhaps most helpful, to categorize these perpetrators with respect to their motivation. When we do, three distinct subgroups emerge: ethnoreligious hatred, domestic issues, and unknown motives. Perpetrators motivated by ethnoreligious hatred had grievances against the world and targeted a specific group of people (e.g., Jews, African-Americans) that they blamed for their problems. This type of mass shooter is usually not known by the congregation. A third of these perpetrators fall into this category.

Those motivated by domestic issues targeted a church because a girlfriend, wife, or other family member happened to be worshiping there.

This type of mass shooter is usually known by the congregation. A third of these perpetrators fall into this category.

The motivations of the final one-third of perpetrators were unknown.

IMPULSIVE AGGRESSION

Violence is a phenomenon that is expressed primarily in two forms: Premeditated violence, like mass shootings, are planned acts in which the perpetrator has the conscious intent to kill or permanently injure another person. In contrast, impulsive aggression is a spontaneous or explosive response to some real or perceived provocation, with a loss of behavioral control. Unlike premeditated violence, impulsive aggression can vary in intensity from minor acts, such as yelling or screaming, to severe violence, such as stabbing, shooting, or killing.[10]

During an impulsive aggressive outburst, a person loses control of his anger and lashes out. Often he will show genuine remorse after the outburst and vow "never to do it again." The frequency of these outbursts can vary from a few times a month to several times a day. Between outbursts, the person may appear normal and well controlled. Impulsive aggressive individuals are often described by family and friends as hot-headed, quick-tempered, or full of rage.[11] Impulsive aggressive outbursts can be symptomatic of several *DSM-5* mental disorders, including attention-deficit/hyperactivity disorder (ADHD), borderline personality disorder, post-traumatic stress disorder (PTSD), bipolar disorder, and substance use disorder.[12] A pastoral counselor is far more likely to encounter individuals involved in instances of impulsive aggression than in premeditated violence.

ASSESSING THE RISK OF VIOLENCE

Predicting a complex behavior, such as violence, is difficult at best. But as with suicidality, violence risk is based on the presence or absence of known risk factors. Risk factors may be static (unchanging), such as gender or a history of violence against others, or they may be dynamic, such as the

Violence at Home

For families struggling to care for a mentally ill loved one who displays violence, life is often frightening and chaotic. The body of Christ provides a place of peace in the midst of turmoil for these families. Continually remind them that at the heart of the gospel is the miracle of transformation: the dead brought to life and the old made new. Change is possible; God is at work in the storm.

SUGGESTED SCRIPTURES

Galatians 5:19–21   Fits of rage are a sinful act of the flesh.

Ephesians 4:30–31   Violence among believers grieves the Holy Spirit.

Colossians 3:8–10   God can renew the hearts of those who perpetrate violence.

BIBLICAL STORY TO CONNECT

The Violent Son

Ezekiel 18:10–13   Those who perpetrate violence, even as a result of mental illness, must be held accountable and appreciate the consequences of their actions.

presence of an emotionally aroused state. To accurately assess the risk of violence, you will likely need to gather information from the client as well as from collateral sources (e.g., a spouse). An individual's risk of violence increases as the number of positive risk factors increases. The following are risk factors that should be considered when assessing a counselee's risk of violence.

History of Violence. Individuals who have been convicted of a violent crime or have acted aggressively in the past are more likely than others to become violent again. Research suggests that this risk factor is the single best predictor of future violence.[13]

Personality Disorders. Impulsive aggression or violence is often a symptom of borderline personality disorder and antisocial personality disorder. When a personality disorder occurs in conjunction with another mental disorder, the combination increases an individual's risk of violent behavior.[14]

Age. The majority of violent crime in the United States is perpetrated by individuals eighteen to thirty-four years old. Among patients in acute psychiatric settings, younger age has been shown to be a consistent predictor of violent behavior.

Gender. From adolescence on, women are significantly less likely than men to report engaging in assaultive behavior and to be arrested for or convicted of violent crimes.[15] For example, men are the perpetrators in 90 percent of all homicides in the United States. This same gender difference in violence has been shown among people with serious mental illness.

Early Exposure. An individual's risk of violence rises with exposure to aggressive family fights during childhood; physical abuse by a parent; or a parent, particularly a father, who was a substance abuser or a convicted criminal. Exposure to violence in childhood is also predictive of mental health problems later in life.

Traumatic Brain Injury. Aggression following traumatic brain injury (TBI) is common. A TBI may compromise important neurological functions involved in emotional regulation and behavioral control, increasing an individual's risk of violence. Research finds that individuals who have experienced a TBI are four times more likely to commit a violent crime than people who have not.[16]

Treatment Noncompliance. Several clinical studies have found a significant relationship between treatment noncompliance and violent acts in individuals with serious mental illness. It has been suggested that a lack of insight into one's mental illness leads to treatment noncompliance, which results in an exacerbation of psychiatric symptoms and an associated increase in the risk of violence.

Social Stress. People with high levels of social stress (e.g., poverty, homelessness, overcrowding) are more likely than others to become violent. Individuals experiencing significant social stress report higher levels of hopelessness, fatalism, and lack of control over their circumstances. Prolonged exposure to high levels of social stress has been shown to damage areas of the brain, such as the prefrontal cortex, that are involved in emotional regulation and behavioral control.

Anger. Anger is a normal emotional state that occurs when an individual perceives that her interests have been violated or disrespected by another. Anger becomes maladaptive when it is underregulated, chronically accessible, and has a low threshold of occurrence. In individuals with serious mental illness, anger has been shown to be predictive of physical aggression both before and during hospital admission as well as after discharge.[17]

Substance Abuse. Research has demonstrated a general association between substance abuse, criminality, and violence. Individuals with a dual diagnosis (substance use disorder plus serious mental illness) are more likely than those with serious mental illness alone to become violent.

Delusions. The presence of paranoid or persecutory delusions (i.e., a false belief that one is being threatened or controlled by forces outside oneself) has been associated with an increased risk of violence. This type of delusional thinking can occur in a variety of disorders, including schizophrenia, depression, bipolar disorder, and dementia.

Violent Command Hallucinations. A command hallucination is a type of auditory hallucination in which "voices" instruct a person to act in a specific way. Some individuals with serious mental illness experience command hallucinations with violent content, in which they are instructed to harm others. Clinical studies have found these individuals to be at a significantly higher risk of violence.[18]

Violent Thoughts. Individuals with persistent violent fantasies of revenge against others for perceived wrongs, a morbid interest in past mass shootings, or involvement in violent extremist groups online are at an increased risk of violence. This is particularly true if an individual also has easy access to guns.

Personal Stress. Unemployment, financial strain, divorce, or separation in the past year increases an individual's risk of violence. Research finds that high levels of personal stress play a significant role in workplace violence and spousal abuse.[19]

Suicidality and Self-Harm. Suicidal threats, suicide attempts, and nonfatal deliberate self-harm have all been shown to be associated with an increased risk of violence. It has been suggested that the emotional dysregulation associated with these harmful behaviors makes the individual susceptible to impulsive aggressive outbursts.[20]

Emotional Arousal. Individuals rarely display aggressive behavior when their emotions are well controlled. The presence of high emotional arousal has been associated with an increased risk of impulsive aggression. A highly agitated or irritable state usually precedes an impulsive aggressive outburst. In this emotionally aroused state, the individual is typically anxious, angry, easily annoyed, and has trouble sitting still.[21]

STAYING SAFE

The most common setting for pastoral counseling places you alone, in a confined space, with an individual whose level of emotional disturbance is not necessarily known at the start. While it is unlikely that a counselee will become aggressive, it is always best to be proactive and err on the side of caution. So in addition to conducting an initial assessment to determine each client's potential for violence, consider the following safety issues to reduce your risk of physical assault and harassment.

Minimize Personal Information. To minimize the risks of stalking, cyberbullying, and harassment, protect your privacy if you use social and business media (e.g., Twitter, Facebook, LinkedIn). In your office, minimize the presence of personal possessions that contain identifying details.

Many pastoral counselors also choose to have their phone number and home address unlisted in local directories.

Create Entry Procedures. Counselees should always have an appointment to be on the church campus. They should also be required to check in at the church's front desk. Staff at the front desk should call you to confirm the appointment and then show the person to your office.

Remove Potential Weapons. Do not have anything accessible in your office that could be used as a weapon, such as a letter opener or heavy paperweight. Choose chairs and tables that are too heavy to be picked up and thrown.

Give Yourself an Exit. Position office furniture in such a way that you are closer to the door than the counselee, so that you can quickly exit if necessary.

Be Able to Call for Help. Some churches provide pastoral counselors with "panic buttons" that alert other staff to a dangerous situation. If that is not available and you are concerned that there is a serious risk of violence with a particular counselee, keep your door open slightly, so that other staff will hear if something starts to happen.

Make an Excuse to Exit. If a counselee becomes agitated and won't calm down, get out of the room by saying you need to use the bathroom or that you forgot to give a staff member a message. Have your exit excuse prepared and rehearsed before it is needed.

Avoid Working Alone. Always make sure someone else is around when you are working with clients. Do not see counselees at the church in the early morning or late evening when everyone else is gone.

PASTORAL CARE AFTER VIOLENCE

In the aftermath of violence, the role of the pastoral counselor is to support and protect family members or others who may be involved from further harm while developing a process by which the violent individual might be restored. The following is a five-step process for pastoral care following a violent act.

1. In the presence of the violent individual, identify the violent behavior and describe the associated consequences. Let the person know that violence toward others is a sinful act that simply will not be tolerated and that whenever violent or threatening behavior is displayed, the police will be called. The violent individual must be separated from the family for a period of time, to safeguard others and to allow for protective measures to be put in place. This may mean hospitalization or arrest for the perpetrator or, in the case of domestic violence, temporary accommodations for the wife and children.

2. Help the family to avoid enabling the person's violent behavior. The common response to an aggressive outburst is to back down and avoid the circumstance or topic that triggered the incident. As a result, families often "walk on eggshells" around the person, and the problem is never dealt with or brought to light. This "avoid the issue at all costs" response actually reinforces the idea that violence is an effective way to get what you want and makes it more likely to happen again. Instead, the individual must be held accountable for his actions, either by the criminal justice system, the church, the family, or a combination of parties.

3. Allow the individual to suffer the full consequences of his violent behavior. The individual must understand the gravity of his behavior. If the family constantly covers for him or minimizes the negative consequences of his behavior (e.g., posts bail, lies for him), the potential for change is greatly limited.

4. Emphasize that restoration and forgiveness are possible in Christ. While violent behavior may permanently damage a person's relationships with family members and loved ones, nothing can separate him from the love of Christ (Rom. 8:39). "In him we have redemption through his blood, the forgiveness of sins" (Eph. 1:7). The family may struggle to forgive and accept him again, but God's love is unconditional and freely given.

5. Help the family to set up appropriate boundaries within the home. Behavior does not change overnight. If a violent person returns to the family, he will need to be guided toward relational restoration. Clear and appropriate boundaries will help the family guide and monitor his progress. This will be a long and difficult process for the family. Encourage them to reward successes while pointing out failures in an environment of love and acceptance.

Community Mental Health Resources

I n an earlier chapter, you read the story of Oscar, a missionary struggling with severe depression and anxiety. Considering his mental health problems to be primarily spiritual in nature, Oscar initially sought help from his pastor, William. Unbeknownst to Oscar, the connections and relationships that William had developed with local mental health-care providers long before Oscar came in would play a significant role in his recovery.

Years earlier, when William had begun practicing as a pastoral counselor, he quickly realized that many of his congregants required professional mental health treatment in addition to his pastoral services. Concerned about referring to mental health-care providers he didn't know or have a relationship with, he began meeting, mostly over lunch, with local providers. During those meetings, he would learn about the provider's practice, training, and types of insurance accepted. He would also ask how the provider felt about working with religious clients. In addition, he would explain the types of services he offered as a pastoral counselor and find out whether the provider would be willing to work collaboratively with him to help clients he might refer.

Over time William was able to develop strong personal and professional relationships with a large number of psychiatrists, licensed counselors, and clinical psychologists who he felt could benefit his more seriously ill counselees. It was during one of those lunch meetings that William first met Lisa, the clinical psychologist he referred Oscar to for therapy. During lunch, William learned that Lisa used a cognitive-behavioral therapy approach and considered treating depression one of her specialties. She also shared that she was a Christian, even though she did not advertise herself as a Christian psychologist or overtly integrate faith into therapy. Following that meeting, William and Lisa were successful at working collaboratively with several clients, and William eventually referred Oscar to her for therapy. While Oscar was initially resistant to seeing a "secular psychologist," he was put at ease by the fact that William knew Lisa to be a Christian and had worked collaboratively with her in the past.

A STARTING POINT FOR CARE

Individuals and families dealing with serious mental illness typically feel lost about where to find help. Time and again, they ask the same frustrating question: "Where do we start?" Their confusion and sense of helplessness have no precedent. Friends and extended family members often offer little in the way of support or understanding for disorders that are generally stigmatized and misunderstood, and the search for effective resources, treatment facilities, and programs is often a haphazard process of trial and error.

Like most people, pastors often have few, if any, relationships with mental health-care providers and are also unclear about exactly where to start when a congregant needs care.[1] This lack of connection to trusted providers in the community causes many pastoral counselors to take on counselees with problems that far exceed their training and expertise.[2] And although a collaborative team approach better serves the afflicted, strangely, many pastors feel they have to do it alone.

This chapter will make you aware of the mental health resources available in most communities, outline a process by which you might build collaborative relationships with local mental health-care providers, and describe the steps involved in making a successful referral. As an informed advocate, you will be an encouragement and a blessing to hurting families struggling to find care for mentally ill loved ones.

The Lord Will Provide (Jehovah Jireh)

As part of his loving providence toward us, God has given us resources that can reduce or limit the psychological suffering we endure as a result of living in a fallen world. These resources include medication, physicians, psychologists, and counselors. When believers access these and similar mental health resources, they are simply reaping the benefits of God's provision for us.

SUGGESTED SCRIPTURES

Matthew 6:31–33	God knows our every need and will provide for us.
Romans 8:28	All things work together for good, for those who love God.
James 1:17	Every good and perfect gift comes from God our Father.

BIBLICAL STORY TO CONNECT

King Hezekiah

2 Kings 20:1–7	Whether healing occurs miraculously or through a physical remedy, God is always the source.

CRISIS RESOURCES

As a pastoral counselor, it is important to effectively assess the magnitude of a situation before you act. The most significant distinction you must make is whether you are dealing with a crisis or a problem. A *crisis* involves an immediate safety concern for you or another (e.g., suicidal thoughts or behaviors) and requires the involvement of emergency personnel to be resolved. A *problem* is not an emergency and can be managed or addressed over time. In the event that you are dealing with a crisis, it will be important for you to be familiar with the following community resources:

Welfare Check—If you or someone you know is worried about an individual living with mental illness and cannot reach him, call the non-emergency number for the police department in your community, explain your concern, and ask them to conduct a welfare check.

National Suicide Prevention Lifeline—The Suicide Prevention Lifeline is not only for individuals considering self-harm; it is also for those who need to talk about or receive guidance in responding to another's suicidal thoughts or behaviors. Call 800-273-TALK (8255) or go to www.suicide preventionlifeline.org for a live online chat. The Lifeline is available twenty-four hours a day, seven days a week.

Mental Health Crisis Clinic or Hospital Emergency Room—If an individual is in immediate danger of harming herself or others, she needs to be seen by a mental health-care provider. Many communities have specialized mental health-crisis clinics for situations such as this. When a crisis clinic is unavailable, a hospital emergency room is your best option. Making contact with the educational specialist or community liaison at your local crisis clinic or hospital, so that you can learn the process that occurs when a suicidal individual is brought there, will help you to comfort and inform families when a crisis occurs.

911 Emergency Services—If a situation is life-threatening, do not hesitate to call 911 to ask for immediate assistance. Tell the operator that someone is experiencing a mental health crisis and explain the nature of the emergency. Understand that once the police or other emergency personnel arrive, you no longer control the situation. You can and should encourage officers to view the situation as a mental health crisis, not a crime, but you must not interfere with first responders in the performance of their duties.

Mental Health Deputies—Mental health deputies are police officers specially trained in crisis intervention. They help resolve the immediate mental health crisis and link the individual to the appropriate resources for ongoing assistance. Not all communities offer this advanced service, so you will need to determine whether it exists in your area by calling your local police or sheriff's department.

Crisis Intervention Team—A crisis intervention team (CIT) includes both a mental health-care provider and a specially trained police officer. This team is dispatched into the community following a 911 call to provide emergency care to a person experiencing a mental health crisis. CITs traditionally provide crisis assessment and then link the distressed individual to psychiatric treatment and other services in the community. Follow-up after the crisis is common to make sure the individual is receiving outpatient services. Not all communities offer this advanced service, so you will need to determine whether it exists in your area by calling your local police or sheriff's department.

Mental Health Warrant—A mental health warrant authorizes law-enforcement officers to take into custody a person who shows a serious need for help with a mental illness and who is in immediate and serious risk of harm to self or others. The warrant orders the person in custody to undergo a mental health evaluation by a doctor to determine whether hospitalization (i.e., involuntary commitment) is necessary. To obtain a mental health warrant, a family member must provide current and specific information that shows the prospective patient is suffering from a mental illness and constitutes an immediate danger to himself or others. This type of extreme action is often sought by families who have a mentally ill loved one who lacks insight into his illness and refuses treatment. Most often, a mental health warrant is issued by the county attorney's office, but this varies from state to state. Knowing the process for obtaining a mental health warrant will significantly aid families with a loved one who is in danger of self-harm and is refusing treatment.

Guardianship—Due to the debilitating effects of serious mental illness, some adults become unable to care for themselves and require help managing their daily affairs. One way to help them manage their lives is through a legal guardianship. A guardianship is a relationship between a ward and a guardian that is established by a court of law. A ward is an individual who is deemed incapacitated by the court. It is important to understand that a diagnosis of mental illness alone is not conclusive evidence for the finding of incapacity; instead, a court will look at the individual's pattern of behavior and judgments, paired with medical information, to assess the degree of incapacity. A guardianship should always be viewed as a last resort in the care of a person living with mental illness.

MENTAL HEALTH-CARE PROVIDERS

The licensed mental health professionals available to help individuals diagnosed with psychiatric conditions can widely differ in type and level of training. Knowing which provider is the best referral for a particular congregant can be confusing, but becoming familiar with the various types of mental health-care providers can help.

Licensed Professional Counselor (LPC)—This professional is trained to evaluate a person's mental health and to use talk therapy (psychotherapy) to treat psychological distress. An LPC has a master's degree in a mental health–related field such as psychology, counseling, or educational psychology.

Licensed Marriage and Family Therapist (LMFT)—A marriage and family therapist offers guidance on problem interpersonal issues. The therapist looks at behavior within a social/relational framework and focuses almost solely on couples and families. An LMFT has a master's degree in marriage and family therapy.

Licensed Clinical Social Worker (LCSW)—Social workers are the largest group of clinically trained mental health service providers. Like an LPC, a licensed clinical social worker is trained to evaluate a person's mental health and to use talk therapy to treat psychological distress. The social worker is also trained in case management and advocacy services. An LCSW has a master's degree in social work.

Licensed Chemical Dependency Counselor (LCDC)—A chemical dependency counselor provides guidance and support to individuals recovering from substance use disorders. An LCDC has an associate's degree or higher in substance abuse treatment.

Clinical Psychologist—A clinical psychologist is trained in the diagnosis of mental and behavioral health problems as well as in talk therapy. A psychologist is more likely to work with individuals who have serious mental illnesses than are professionals who identify themselves as counselors. A clinical psychologist has either a doctor of philosophy (PhD) degree in clinical psychology or a doctor of psychology (PsyD) degree.

Psychiatrist—A psychiatrist is a medical doctor who is trained in how the brain works and can prescribe medications to treat mental disorders. Few psychiatrists are still trained to use talk therapy in their practices. A psychiatrist has either a doctor of medicine (MD) or doctor of osteopathic medicine (DO) degree.

ONLINE PROVIDER SEARCH ENGINES

A number of national provider databases are available online that allow you to search for mental health-care professionals by city or zip code. These include search engines developed by the American Association of Christian Counselors (connect.aacc.net/?search_type=distance), Focus on the Family (christiancounselors.network/), the American Psychiatric Association (finder .psychiatry.org/), the American Psychological Association (locator.apa.org/), and *Psychology Today* (therapists: psychologytoday.com/us/therapists; psychiatrists: psychologytoday.com/us/psychiatrists). In addition, calling 211 from anywhere in the United States will put you in touch with a referral specialist who can help you find mental health resources in your area. The 211 system is available twenty-four hours a day, seven days a week, and can also be accessed online at 211.org.

SCREENING PROVIDERS

The important work of making connections with trusted mental health-care providers in your community must be done long before the counselee is sitting in your office. To get started, ask physicians and mental health-care providers in your congregation who they refer to in the community.

When building relationships with providers, seek out professionals who are willing to work collaboratively with you. Psychologist Mark McMinn has identified seven principles of effective clergy-psychologist collaboration:[3]

1. **Relationship.** Successful clergy-psychologist collaborations take place in the context of personal relationships.
2. **Communication.** Without good communication, relationships deteriorate. Clear consistent communication is a must, whether it means becoming familiar with spiritual terms or understanding psychiatric diagnoses.
3. **Respect.** Relationships must be founded on mutual respect. Feedback is one form of communication, and responding to it well is one way of demonstrating respect.

4. **Common values and goals.** Collaboration thrives in the presence of shared values, especially common respect for religious ideals, and it is strangled by value conflicts on important issues.

5. **Complementary expertise.** Collaborative relationships must be grounded in the knowledge that each professional has something unique and valuable to offer. A willingness to ask for help and admit limitations is also important, for without need, what is to be gained from collaboration?

6. **Psychological and spiritual mindedness.** Individuals who understand both cultural mindsets, psychological and spiritual, are best prepared for collaboration.

7. **Trust.** All of these things taken together build trust. As trust is built over time, opportunities for further collaboration will increase.

Research consistently finds that pastors are most comfortable referring to mental health-care providers who are Christians.[4] This is a particularly high threshold, given the present shortage of providers. In addition, many providers may be people of faith who simply do not advertise themselves that way (i.e., as Christian counselors) or do not overtly integrate biblical principles into their particular psychotherapeutic approach. So when screening mental health-care providers, it is imperative to determine whether they will be sensitive to spiritual issues that may arise when treating believers and whether they are affirming of the Christian faith.

As you look at potential referrals, you must also gather information on their costs and the types of insurance they accept. For congregants without financial resources, seek out providers who charge on a sliding scale or who are willing to offer limited *pro bono* services. Local universities or colleges that offer graduate programs in psychology or counseling may have clinics where students provide mental health services for a reduced fee. Most states and counties provide some system to care for the mental health of those who lack financial resources. Find out how to engage these systems in your area by calling your state's Department of Health and Human Services.

MAKING A REFERRAL

A referral to a mental health professional with whom you have a personal relationship is often meaningful to the person being referred. As such, a referral should never be seen as "passing the buck" or as sending the individual away to "get fixed"; rather, it should be seen as a collaborative opportunity in which the pastoral counselor, family members, and mental health-care provider work as a team, to care for and support the struggling person in pursuit of healing. Take the following steps to make a successful mental health referral.

1. Express Your Concern. If, after talking with and assessing a counselee, you believe that a mental health problem may be present, express your concern. Affirm the person for seeking assistance and taking the first step toward healing. Stay away from the use of diagnostic terms like depression or anxiety disorder, and simply state that you believe the problem requires mental health resources in addition to pastoral counseling.

2. Explain Your Role. Explain that your role as a pastoral counselor is to provide a framework for processing life's situations using prayer, spiritual guidance, and biblical wisdom. Help him to understand that your role will not change if he also sees a mental health-care provider. Ensure that you will continue to meet with him for pastoral care and to work collaboratively with the mental health-care provider on his case.

It is often also helpful to discuss with the counselee that God has created multiple aspects to our being (i.e., physical, mental, spiritual, and relational) and that intervention that focuses solely on a single aspect of that being can bring limited relief at best. A holistic approach, however, is comprehensive, addressing the whole individual. God has lovingly provided experts with knowledge of the differing aspects of our beings to help reduce our pain and suffering when mental health problems arise.

3. Expect Resistance. Generally, people are not open to seeking assistance from mental health-care providers. This resistance to care is primarily driven by the negative attitudes and discrimination (i.e., the stigma) commonly directed toward those with mental health problems.[5] Stigma is born out of fear and misinformation and can only be overcome by truth and education. So help the resistant person understand that a mental health problem results from a combination of biological, psychological, and environmental influences and not from a weakness in character or faith. Assure the person that there is no reason to be ashamed. If the individual continues to refuse a mental health referral, a secondary option is to request that she make an appointment with her primary care physician (PCP) for a complete physical with blood work. Encourage her to speak with the PCP about the same issues for which she sought your counsel. This will help rule out physical problems that may be mimicking a mental health issue (e.g., hypothyroidism) and potentially give you a professional ally who will also suggest a mental health referral.

4. Explore Barriers to Access. To increase the likelihood that a referral will be successful, it is important that you discuss with the counselee any barriers that may limit his ability to access mental health care. Barriers to accessing care, as discussed in an earlier chapter, can include a lack of transportation, financial resources, and health insurance coverage.

5. Engage the Mental Health-Care Provider. Using the information you have gathered, find the best match for the congregant from your list of screened mental health-care providers. If possible, have her make an appointment from your office before she leaves.

6. Follow Up. At your next pastoral counseling session, inquire about his appointment with the referred mental health professional. If he does not have another pastoral counseling session scheduled, call him to make sure he kept the appointment with the referred provider. If you find that he did not attend or that he canceled the appointment, encourage him to reschedule.

AFFORDABLE PSYCHIATRIC MEDICATION

For many individuals living with serious mental illness, psychiatric medication is an important part of treatment. Unfortunately, for those without prescription drug coverage, these medications are often prohibitively expensive. To help those who are struggling to afford their medication, a number of prescription-assistance programs exist, including NeedyMeds (needymeds.org/), RxAssist (rxassist.org/), Patient Assistance (patientassistance.com/), and GoodRx (goodrx.com/).

RESIDENTIAL TREATMENT FACILITIES

Familiarize yourself with the psychiatric hospitals and residential addiction treatment facilities in your area. A good place to start is the Substance Abuse and Mental Health Services Administration's (SAMHSA) online behavioral health treatment services locator (findtreatment.samhsa.gov/). Or call the SAMHSA national helpline at 800-662-HELP (4357). SAMHSA provides referrals to local treatment facilities, support groups, and community-based mental health organizations.

HIPAA

In the instance that you find yourself collaborating with a mental healthcare provider, be aware that you cannot share client information with that provider unless the counselee signs a release-of-information form. This is due to the Health Insurance Portability and Accountability Act (HIPAA), a federal law that helps protect the privacy of individuals' health information. HIPAA was signed into law by President Bill Clinton on August 21, 1996. The Office of Civil Rights at the federal Department of Health and Human Services (HHS) has enforcement authority over HIPAA.

While the protection of a person's health information is important and necessary, HIPAA causes unique problems for the caregivers of adults with serious mental illness, particularly those who may be delusional or paranoid. For example, if an adult child (over eighteen years) objects to the release of information by her psychiatrist and then receives medication from or schedules a follow-up appointment with that psychiatrist, then her parent or caregiver, according to HIPAA, cannot be given the information that they may need to ensure that she takes the medication or attends the next appointment.

While HIPAA does contain provisions that allow information to be shared, providers and institutions tend to default to nondisclosure even when the law permits disclosure. HIPAA allows a mental health-care provider to share information with a caregiver if the patient agrees (or does not object), if the caregiver is the patient's legal personal representative (e.g., legal guardian), if the mental health-care provider determines that the patient does not have the capacity to make health-care decisions,[6] or if the caregiver can help prevent or lessen a threat of harm to the patient or others. HIPAA also does not prohibit caregivers from sharing information with mental health-care providers that they believe might be relevant or helpful; therefore, caregivers should do so if possible. HIPAA does not require a mental health-care provider to disclose information they receive privately from a caregiver with the patient.

Familiarizing yourself with HIPAA and knowing where to direct families for information (https://www.hhs.gov/hipaa/for-individuals/mental-health/index.html) will prove tremendously helpful to them as they navigate the mental health-care system.

RESOURCES FOR VETERANS

Many veterans of the armed services receive their mental health care through the Veterans Administration (VA), so it is important that you familiarize yourself with the VA mental health services available in your local community. A good place to direct veterans and their families in distress is the Veterans Crisis Line, which can be accessed at 800-273-8255 (option 1) or online at VeteransCrisisLine.net.

SUPPORT GROUPS

There is strong evidence for the clinical efficacy of peer-led support groups in mental health recovery.[7] So become familiar with organizations in your area that offer mental health support groups (e.g., the National Alliance for the Mentally Ill at www.nami.org; the Depression/Bipolar Support Alliance at www.dbsalliance.org; the Alzheimer's Association at www.alz.org; Alcoholics Anonymous at www.aa.org). Support groups are beneficial not only for individuals who are living with mental illness but for their caregivers as well.

RURAL SETTINGS

For clergy in rural settings where mental health-care providers and services may not be available, referrals to primary care physicians and the use of telepsychiatry/psychology are important options. When no mental health-care providers exist in an area, primary care physicians can be used to provide needed psychiatric medications, so you should screen primary care physicians in your area as potential mental health referral options.

Telepsychiatry/psychology takes advantage of technologies such as the internet or smartphones to provide mental health services electronically to the client. As an advocate for families struggling with mental health-care problems, you should become familiar with companies that provide these services, such as AmWell (amwell.com/cm/), Doctor on Demand (doctorondemand.com/), and TalkSpace (talkspace.com/).

GOVERNMENT ENTITLEMENT PROGRAMS

Individuals with mental illness may not be able to work or may have trouble holding jobs. This becomes particularly difficult when they are the primary providers in their families. Fortunately, these individuals are often eligible for government assistance, through entitlement programs such as Supplemental Security Income (SSI). SSI is a federal income-supplement program designed to help aged, blind, and disabled people who have little or no income. It provides cash in a monthly stipend to help individuals meet basic needs for food, clothing, and shelter. Information about the program can be found on the Social Security Administration website at (www.ssa.gov/ssi/).

Eligible individuals may also be able to access mental health services through Medicaid. States vary, however, in what types of mental health services they provide under Medicaid. Use the following database to find what Medicaid benefits are available in your state: kff.org/data-collection /medicaid-benefits/.

Finally, children who don't have health insurance are very often eligible for state medical coverage. Insurance is available to children in working families, including families with a variety of immigration statuses. To find out what your state's policies are, what's covered, and how to apply, call 877-543-7669 or find your state at www.insurekidsnow.gov/state/index .html.

HOUSING

For individuals living with mental health challenges, finding safe and affordable housing can be difficult. As a pastoral counselor, you will likely be approached by individuals and families looking for two types of housing: immediate and long-term. To help with immediate housing needs, you will need to become familiar with local emergency shelters and missions that serve the homeless.

For long-term needs, the federal government's Department of Housing and Urban Development (HUD) provides a number of housing assistance programs. HUD's Housing Choice Voucher Program, also known as Section 8 housing, assists low-income families, the elderly, and the disabled. Another HUD program offers low-income renters the opportunity to pay 30 percent of their gross adjusted income for housing and utilities; the landlord then receives a voucher from the federal government that covers the remainder of the rent.

The Supportive Housing for People with Disabilities Program, also known as Section 811, is a federal program dedicated to developing and subsidizing rental housing for extremely low-income adults with disabilities, such as those who have chronic mental illness. The biggest difference between this program and similar ones is that it provides housing specifically for the disabled and, as such, ensures that all housing has access to appropriate supportive services, like case management and employment assistance. Information on both of these programs can be found on the HUD website at www.hud.gov.

MENTAL HEALTH GATEWAY

The Mental Health Gateway is an online resource designed to provide pastoral counselors with the information, tools, and resources they need to effectively assist individuals who need help with mental health difficulties. The website (www.mentalhealthgateway.org) is organized by mental disorder and includes short educational videos and a step-by-step guide to assist you in finding and referring an individual to mental health resources in your local community.

Relationship

Religious and Spiritual Factors

Marcus is a twenty-year-old college sophomore who recently returned from a spring break mission trip to Central America. One Saturday afternoon, I received a frantic phone call from his roommate Steve. Steve explained that Marcus had been kneeling in his room, hands raised, praying loudly in an unintelligible voice for the past six hours. He would not stop or respond, even though Steve had tried to engage him several times. I asked him when Marcus's odd behavior had begun.

Steve explained that they had returned from a mission trip two weeks earlier. During the trip, he had noticed that Marcus was more animated and energetic than normal. Marcus also began saying that he was hearing from God in new and deeper ways. At the time, this did not seem strange, because many of the students on the trip were reporting personal religious experiences and spiritual growth. Once they returned, however, Marcus's behavior became even more strange. He would fast for days, something he had never done before, and he would say that he was receiving new revelation from the Holy Spirit. Marcus believed that God was calling him to quit school and leave for the mission field immediately. Steve said, "At first

I thought it was just religious zeal from the mission trip, but every day, he would say God was calling him to a completely different country. His behavior was erratic and unpredictable. He even stopped going to class." I asked Steve if Marcus had any mental health problems or used alcohol or drugs. Steve didn't know of any mental health problems and said that Marcus rarely drank alcohol and never used drugs. He did say, however, that he and Marcus were both taking the anti-malarial drug mefloquine.

The mission trip Marcus and Steve had gone on was to a region of Central America where malaria transmission is common, so all the students were prescribed mefloquine before the trip as a preventive measure. The normal administration protocol for mefloquine in such cases is to take one dose per week starting two weeks before traveling and then one dose per week while in the area of malaria risk and for four consecutive weeks after returning home. At this point, Marcus had been taking mefloquine for five weeks.

What Steve did not know is that psychosis is a rare but known side effect of mefloquine in some people.[1] Marcus was likely experiencing religious delusions and hallucinations as a result of the medication. I explained this to Steve and asked him to take Marcus to the emergency room. The emergency room physician stopped Marcus's mefloquine and gave him an injection of an antipsychotic medication along with a prescription for the same. Since he was not a danger to himself or others, Marcus was sent home with a referral to a local psychiatrist. Steve and I notified Marcus's parents, and they drove to town the next day to care for him. It took about a month before Marcus's thoughts and behavior fully returned to normal.

HYPER-RELIGIOSITY

Hyper-religiosity, like that displayed by Marcus, is a pathological form of religious behavior so extreme that it interferes with a person's normal functioning. These abnormal religious experiences and beliefs are inconsistent with those accepted by the individual's religious tradition or faith community. Hyper-religiosity occurs in patients with neurological conditions (e.g., temporal lobe epilepsy, brain tumors) or psychiatric conditions and is primarily expressed in two ways: as (1) religious delusions and hallucinations, or (2) scrupulosity.

Religious Delusions and Hallucinations. Delusions are strongly held false beliefs despite the presentation of clear evidence to the contrary, while hallucinations are sensory experiences in which the person reports seeing, hearing, smelling, tasting, or feeling something that is not actually present. Delusions with religious themes (e.g., receiving special revelation from God, believing God has chosen you for a special mission) are common, accounting for approximately one-third of all delusional experiences in psychiatric patients.[2] Similarly, it is estimated that a quarter of all reported hallucinations are religious in nature (e.g., hearing the voice of God, seeing the devil or demons). Schizophrenia and bipolar disorder (during a manic episode) are the mental illnesses most commonly associated with religious delusions and hallucinations.

Scrupulosity. Obsessive-compulsive disorder (OCD) is characterized by recurrent thoughts (obsessions) or behaviors (compulsions) that people feel they cannot control. Obsessions are persistent thoughts that a person recognizes as intrusive and inappropriate and that result in heightened anxiety. Compulsions are behaviors that the person performs to try to prevent or stop the anxiety related to the obsessions. Scrupulosity is a subtype of OCD in which the obsessions and compulsions are religious or moral in nature.

Common religious obsessions in scrupulosity include recurrent thoughts that one has committed a sin by mistake or without realizing it, intrusive sacrilegious or blasphemous thoughts or images, doubts that one is faithful or pious enough, fear that one performed a religious ritual or ceremony improperly, and a persistent fear of eternal damnation and punishment from God. Common religious compulsions include excessively praying or reading the Bible, repeating religious rituals until they are performed perfectly, continually seeking unnecessary reassurance from religious leaders or loved ones about spiritual matters, confessing excessively or inappropriately, and avoiding situations in which one believes a religious or moral error would likely occur.

Scrupulosity differs from compulsive religious behavior that may be encouraged or required by a denominational tradition as part of normal worship in two ways. First, the religious obsessions and compulsions take control of the individual's life, making it impossible for him to function normally in at least one area of daily living (i.e., work, school, or relationships). Second, unlike healthy religious practices that are associated with an increase in positive emotions and a decrease in psychological distress, the religious obsessions and compulsions associated with scrupulosity produce overwhelming guilt, fear, and anxiety.

> **Individuals who experience** hyper-religiosity often struggle to distinguish between the spiritual and pathological aspects of their religious experiences. This was true in Marcus's case. While he recognized that the medication had brought on a psychotic episode and hyper-religiosity, he also felt that God had used the experience to speak directly to him and grow his faith. Research finds that most people who have experienced hyper-religiosity endorse a similar mixed medical and spiritual explanation for their experiences. Many also report that these experiences trigger a deeper personal spiritual journey.[3]

Mental health-care providers are often not equipped to address the religious or spiritual problems of patients; nor do they generally feel at ease with the topic. The pastoral counselor, however, is well equipped, and has an important role to play in helping the counselee put these troubling religious experiences into perspective. This is best done by offering nonjudgmental listening, recognizing the importance of the religious experiences to the individual, and providing the individual with biblical wisdom to clarify the faith community's stance on particular issues or beliefs.

DESTRUCTIVE (SINFUL) BEHAVIOR

Many psychiatric disorders (e.g., bipolar disorder) lower the afflicted individual's ability to control their behavior and/or evaluate the consequences of their actions. This leads to an increase in risk-taking and destructive behavior. Destructive (sinful) behaviors commonly associated with serious mental illness include alcohol and drug abuse, excessive spending, self-harm (e.g., cutting), stealing/shoplifting, and sexual promiscuity.

As a pastoral counselor, it is important for you to help the family understand that destructive behaviors in their loved one are the result of the mental disorder, not the person. These behaviors stem from brain dysfunction and chemical imbalances which lead to distorted thoughts, feelings, and perceptions. The normal reaction is to believe that the person is doing and saying destructive things to harm or disrespect those around him, but behind his negative words and behaviors, he is actually suffering and crying out for help.

Appropriate boundaries must be put into place, to protect the counselee and those in his life. Before you implement new boundaries, you need to discuss and agree with the person's family the consequences for destructive and negative behavior. By setting up and consistently enforcing boundaries for a time, you are providing the afflicted individual with a stable environment rather than allowing the disorder to control his life. The purpose of boundaries is to help the person develop a safe and healthy way of living, not to take away their freedom. The following are suggestions of boundaries you and the family may need to consider if destructive behavior is present.

Substance Abuse. Individuals with serious mental illness are at a higher risk of drug and alcohol abuse. It is advisable to remove alcohol from the home to minimize the temptation to drink. The use of illegal drugs is simply not to be tolerated in the home. Alcohol and drugs alter the delicate balance of chemical transmitters in the brain and make it difficult for psychiatric medications to work effectively.

Attitude and Language. Changes in personality are not uncommon in those struggling with mental illness. The individual may become irritable, explosive, and/or start using foul language. This type of behavior cannot be tolerated, particularly if children are in the home. The use of effective communication can help diffuse difficult interactions and bring calm.

Treatment. Taking prescribed medications and going to scheduled psychiatrist and therapist appointments must also be looked at as a boundary. Organize medications in such a way that they can be taken regularly and with ease. Make arrangements for transportation to all mental health–related appointments.

Finances. When excessive spending is a problem you will need to work out what access the individual has to the family's finances. A good system is a weekly allotted amount of cash or gift certificates. Limit (or bar) access to credit and debit cards. If he is working or receiving an income of some sort, help him create a responsible system for paying bills and savings.

Freedoms and Responsibilities. Depending on the severity of the individual's disorder the family may need to restrict her use of a vehicle, phone, bank account, credit card, and other freedoms around the home and community. This should be seen as a safety issue, not a punishment. For example, Belinda's family grew concerned after she had several car accidents and spent money to excess. Diagnosed six years ago with schizophrenia, Belinda, now thirty, lives alone in an apartment paid for by her parents. Concerned for her safety, her parents decided to sell her car. To allow her the freedom to get around the city they set up an Uber account for her on their credit card. To control her spending they canceled her credit cards, closed out her bank account, and started giving her a small weekly allowance. While initially resistant to these changes, Belinda came to accept them and within weeks they became a normal part of her daily routine.

PASTORAL CARE AND SERIOUS MENTAL ILLNESS

While serious mental illness may alter a person's religious experience, research consistently finds that religious involvement is associated with better overall mental health in those living with a mental disorder.[4] In fact, a

Setting Boundaries

The Bible commands us to control our thoughts and behaviors. In fact, self-control is a fruit of the Spirit. When an individual's emotions and behaviors become out of control due to a mental disorder, boundaries provide the individual an opportunity to regain control. Boundaries can be difficult to establish, but God has called us to speak the truth in love, graciously confront sin, and overcome evil with good.

SUGGESTED SCRIPTURES

Proverbs 24:11	We are to intervene when trouble comes on others.
Proverbs 27:5	Bad behavior should be openly corrected.
Titus 3:10	Boundaries must be monitored with grace.

BIBLICAL STORY TO CONNECT

Gomer

Hosea 1:2–3; 3:1–3	Setting up boundaries is a way of expressing love and care for an individual struggling to control her behavior.

majority of psychiatric patients report that religion is a source of strength and comfort for them and that their faith helps them to cope with their condition.[5] As a pastoral counselor, you have the opportunity to help the counselee build a strong spiritual foundation for recovery.[6] This is best done by focusing on what God has done for us rather than what we must do for him. Three therapeutically beneficial areas of pastoral care for those living with serious mental illness are hope, identity, and purpose.[7]

Hope. In mental health care, hope is the fuel that powers the engine of recovery. Hope is not simply "wishful thinking" that something bad or negative will somehow change. Rather, it is confidently knowing that better things will come despite the present difficulties. For the Christian, true hope is grounded in the person and promises of Christ. As Paul writes in Colossians (1:27), "to them God has chosen to make known among the Gentiles the glorious riches of this mystery, which is Christ in you, the hope of glory." The following are three exercises that can be used to begin to build hope in those suffering with serious mental illness.

Learning to Be Content

Learning to be content in an unpleasant situation, or accepting the current reality, is often the first step toward discovering hope. Accepting one's present circumstances allows a person to move forward in addressing and managing the situation. Acceptance, however, is not agreeing that the current situation is fair or should be happening. Use the following questions to begin a conversation about acceptance for those who have lost hope.

1. What do you feel is the biggest challenge(s) preventing you from having hope?
2. What makes this situation seem impossible?
3. What solutions have you thought of or have others offered?
4. If those suggestions will work, have you tried them?
5. If those suggestions will not (or didn't) work, what would it be like if you were to accept the unpleasant reality?
6. Where do you believe God is in this situation?

Being Thankful

Mental health difficulties bring challenging circumstances. These negative experiences and associated feelings often overshadow the positive aspects of life, causing a person to lose hope. The purpose of this exercise is to promote gratitude. Have the counselee think back on the past day, few days, or week, and remember three to five things they are grateful for. In this way, they are, for a brief time, focusing on good things that have happened to them rather than being overwhelmed by negative thoughts and feelings. Suggest they start a gratitude journal and do this exercise every other day for the next week or two.

Discovering Hope

The following exercise is a way for you to help the counselee with serious mental illness begin to build a foundation of hope, using scripture that can withstand changes in symptoms and circumstances. Review the following statements and verses about the hope we have in Christ with the counselee, discussing each one. Ask them to re-review the statements and verses each morning throughout the week before beginning the day.

I have **HOPE** because Jesus does the following:

- Calls me friend *John 15:15*
- Has overcome the problems of this world *John 16:33*
- Loves me *Romans 5:8*
- Has forgiven me *Colossians 3:13*
- Is in control of all things *Matthew 28:18*
- Is present with me in my struggles *Galatians 2:20*
- Keeps his promises *Philippians 1:6*
- Is unchanging *Hebrews 13:8*
- Has prepared an eternal paradise for me *John 14:3*
- Understands my suffering in regards to the following:
  - Poverty *Matthew 8:20*
  - Rejection *John 6:66*
  - Sorrow *Matthew 26:38*
  - Loneliness *Matthew 27:46*
  - Frustration *John 2:15–16*
  - Ridicule *Mark 15:19*
  - Disappointment *Luke 13:34*

Identity. Individuals living with serious mental illness often feel as if they are little more than a diagnosis. That false and damaging belief is confirmed when they hear people say things like, "He's a schizophrenic" or "She's bipolar." The scriptures, however, say that our true identity, who we really are, is not based on our circumstances, diagnosis, or what other people think of us but rather on who we are in the eyes of our Creator. The following exercises are designed to dispel the myth that the counselee is defined by their disorder and help them recognize that their true identity is in Christ.

Who Am I?

Though we play different roles with different people, having a strong sense of self is important for recovery. Have the counselee draw out how they believe each person below sees them and then discuss the questions.

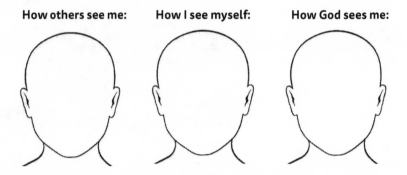

1. What do you notice? Which face portrays your most positive traits?
2. Which face do you wish had more positive traits and how can you make that a reality?
3. How do you think your mental health problems affect others' opinions of you?
4. How has it affected your opinion of yourself?
5. On what do you think God bases his opinion of you?

A Handful of Sand

Christians living with serious mental illness often find it hard to believe that God actually cares about what is going on in their lives. Like most believers, they ask at some point, "Is my life important enough that God would care to take notice of me?" Have the counselee hold a handful of sand and recite/meditate on the following verse; then discuss the questions.

> How precious are your thoughts about me, O God. They cannot be numbered! I can't even count them; they outnumber the grains of sand! And when I wake up, you are still with me! Psalm 139:17–18
>
> 1. What do you find interesting about this verse?
> 2. Why is this hard to believe? How can you make it easier to accept?

How God Sees Me

Below are the scriptural truths that all believers in Christ must continually be reminded of so that we might live out our true identity. Ask the counselee to read aloud the statements below and meditate on these truths throughout the week.

- I was known and chosen by God before the foundation of the world. *Ephesians 1:14*
- I am God's workmanship, his unique masterpiece. *Ephesians 2:10*
- I am a free son/daughter of a loving heavenly Father. *Romans 8:15*
- I am a brand new person; the old, sinful, broken me is dead. *2 Corinthians 5:17*
- I am holy and dearly loved by God; this is my new clothing. *Colossians 3:12*
- I have been redeemed and forgiven by God's grace. *Ephesians 1:7*

- I am a temple, where God's life and love dwell. *1 Corinthians 6:19*
- Christ himself lives in me, and he is always present with me. *Colossians 1:27*
- I have been given the mind of Christ to know his loving thoughts. *1 Corinthians 2:16*
- I am never separated from him because I have direct access to him. *Ephesians 2:18*
- God never has and will never condemn me. *Romans 8:1*
- I have been given the spirit of wisdom and revelation to know him. *Ephesians 1:17*
- I am a member and significant part of Christ's body. *1 Corinthians 12:27*
- I am called a friend by Jesus. *John 15:15*
- I have been made complete in Christ. *Colossians 2:10*

Purpose. God's purpose for us is to have a life-giving relationship with him. In addition, he has created each of us with unique skills, gifts, and talents for the good works he has laid out before us. Since God is good, his purposes and plans for us are also good. Likewise, since he is the one who sets our paths, no person's purpose is more or less important than another's; they are all part of God's greater plan. Mental illness does not hinder God's purposes nor does it alter God's plan for a person's life. God has given each of us, even those with serious mental illness, different talents and spiritual gifts so that we might be equipped to fulfill the specific purpose and plan he has ordained for our life. The purpose of the following exercises is to help the counselee understand how God has wired her so that she might live out his purpose and plan for her life.

Our Shared Purpose

At some level, all believers in Christ share a common God-given purpose. We are the beloved children of God, created by our heavenly Father to reflect his glory, walk in his love, and seek his will for our lives. Ask the counselee to read aloud the biblical statements about our shared purpose below and discuss what each means. Use the associated Bible verses to go deeper.

- To display the glory of God *Psalm 8:1-9; 1 Corinthians 10:31*
- To seek the kingdom of God *Psalm 105:4; Matthew 6:33*
- To proclaim the works of God *Ephesians 2:10; Titus 2:14*
- To grow in the knowledge of God *Proverbs 9:10; Colossians 1:10*
- To believe in the Word of God (Jesus) *John 1:1; John 6:29*
- To share the love of God *Luke 10: 7; 1 John 4:8*
- To imitate the Son of God *Romans 8:29-30; 2 Corinthians 3:18*

My Strengths and Talents

As people work to find God's purpose for their life, it is important they see themself from a healthy and positive perspective. Have the counselee answer the following questions and then reflect on these strengths.

- I have a natural talent for _____ .
- People often compliment me about _____ .
- My favorite thing to do is _____ .
- I feel good/peaceful when I _____ .
- The thing I like most about myself is _____ .
- The accomplishment I'm most proud of is _____ .
- The cause I am most passionate about is _____ .

How Has God Wired Me?

The items below can be used as a starting point to help the counselee begin to determine how God has equipped them to live out his purposes here on the earth. Have them spend ten minutes each day doing something from this list. When a person is involved in activities associated with their purpose, they will feel more exhilarated, excited, and alive.

1. **Passions.** List things you do for fun or that you really enjoy.
2. **Talents/Skills.** List talents/skills that you have.
3. **Actions.** List things that you do naturally without thinking about it (e.g., being optimistic).
4. **Role Models**. List the names of three people you admire and state why.

SERIOUS MENTAL ILLNESS AND FAITH

Mental disorders negatively alter an individual's faith, leaving the believer alone and desperate to know God's loving presence. Psychotic and bipolar disorders cause spiritual confusion manifested as hyper-religiosity or destructive behaviors. The hopelessness and worthlessness of depression results in spiritual disconnection, while anxiety and obsessive-compulsive disorders bring overwhelming spiritual fear. In each case, God appears more like an uncaring taskmaster to the afflicted individual than a loving father. The pastoral counselor has an important role to play in helping those with serious mental illness rediscover their true faith so that they might know the love and grace that God so freely provides.

8

Supporting the Caregiver

Family members are often the primary caregivers of their loved ones with mental disorders. The World Health Organization (WHO) estimates that one in four families has at least one member currently suffering from a mental or behavioral health disorder.[1] Unfortunately, our society and mental health-care system offer little support for these caregivers and families. While the individuals suffering with mental illness may not be able or willing to meet with you for pastoral counseling, their family members are often available and in need of encouragement and care.

A few years ago, I met with a desperate father about his twenty-two-year-old daughter, who suffers with severe depression and, at the time, was hospitalized because of a suicide attempt. Below is a note he shared with me. I present this only to show that, oftentimes, simply encouraging a caregiver's faith is what is most needed.

> I've been meaning to write you now for a few weeks, but without focusing on the excuses for why I haven't, I promised myself that prior to the start of Passover tonight, I would. As I shared with you in our

meetings, the past couple of years have been quite a roller coaster for our family, but out of all darkness comes much light. Of the hundreds, perhaps thousands, of people that we have had the great fortune of meeting and working with through Rachel's challenges, you are clearly one of the most special to me. I would venture to say that perhaps you are the one that had the greatest impact on me (and I hope it is only the beginning). In reflecting on the past two years, whenever we were told, "There's nothing more that could be done," I would think of our two meetings... and it would give me such hope and further determination of what can and must be done.

Perhaps, I'm writing today not only because of the promise I made to myself but also because yesterday, Rachel decided to share her story with others. All along, we told her that we respected her wanting to keep private about it and that, if the day came where she ever wanted to share, we would respect and support her in that decision as well. While she didn't have the opportunity to yet meet you, I told her all about our meetings, and it gave her glimmers of hope in her deepest suffering (and it was VERY deep!). As you may recall, without the support of the medical team that was treating her, we decided, at her pleading and multiple requests, that we would bring her home. We knew it would be a gamble, but for her happiness, we felt it was one worth taking. That was eight weeks ago. We tried putting our own program together, and she agreed to go to various therapies and treatments as we would try and construct the one that would be of greatest benefit. While I honestly believe it's nothing short of a miracle, eight weeks later, we are seeing tremendous improvement. The smile that hundreds loved is back, and she's as outgoing and committed to life as she was before the onset. As a family, along with many in our community, we all have a better understanding of mental illness and are working round the clock to do what we can in the reduction of stigma, which will make the care and treatment so much easier to obtain.

I felt that, although you may not have realized it, you gave me such hope and aspiration to continue in the journey of her recovery.

Although I always have had tremendous faith, you enhanced it. So to you and to your family, who permits you to do the holy work that you do, from the bottom of my heart, I say thank you.

When I first met the writer of this letter, Ari, he had lost all hope that his daughter would ever recover. During our times together, we discussed the hope that we have, despite our circumstances, in our good and loving Father. I reminded him that his daughter is a blessing from the Lord and encouraged him to never stop fighting for her recovery. Our meetings were not for therapy but for pastoral care, and they not only strengthened the faith of this father but also helped him to rebuild hope for his tormented daughter. As a pastoral counselor, you have this same kind of opportunity: to lay a foundation for recovery as you minister to the caregivers and families of those suffering with mental illness.

IMPACT ON THE FAMILY

An estimated 8.4 million people in the United States provide some level of care for an adult living with a mental disorder.[2] In addition, the vast majority of psychiatric inpatients are discharged to a family residence.[3] Approximately 35 to 40 percent are discharged to live with a spouse.[4] While many individuals with mental health problems need assistance, the majority of those who require caregiving have been diagnosed with schizophrenia, bipolar disorder, or severe depression.[5]

Caregivers report a variety of problem behaviors by their loved ones. These behaviors cause distress within the family and include argumentativeness, withdrawal and isolation, a lack of communication, the refusal of treatment, threats or harm to self or others, noisiness at night, the lack of a routine or schedule, uncooperativeness, a refusal to do chores, verbal abuse, and unreasonable demands.[6] As such, caregivers are always "on-call" to cope with and manage the day-to-day crises of serious mental illness.

Caring for a loved one with a mental illness takes a substantial toll on marital and family relationships, faith practices, finances, employment, psychological well-being, and physical health. Research finds that spouses who care for a mentally ill husband or wife show increased levels of depression, anxiety, and marital dissatisfaction. Because of the significant strain on this relationship, divorce and separation rates for these marriages are three to four times the national average.[7]

Caring for a mentally ill loved one has also been shown to hinder a family's ability to practice their faith. In a study of families in Christian faith communities, those who cared for a mentally ill loved one scored significantly lower on measures of faith practice and reported praying less often. They were also more likely to report that one or more members of the family did not attend church.[8]

Financial struggles are also common in families caring for mentally ill loved ones. Not only are these families responsible for some or all of the costs of mental health care, but they are also often forced to deal with a loss of income when the afflicted person is a significant wage earner and can no longer work. Families of people with serious mental illness have been found to have worse physical health, to seek more medical care, and to have higher levels of psychological distress than families without a mentally ill loved one.[9] For example, in a recent study, a majority of the parents (62 percent) who cared for an adult child with mental illness reported that their caregiving role had made their own health worse.[10] The deterioration of a family member's physical and emotional health negatively impacts their ability to serve as an effective caregiver. This puts both the caregiver and the loved one at risk of a mental health crisis.

MOVING FROM ENABLING TO EMPOWERING

Enabling is a behavioral pattern that reinforces destructive behavior or harmful choices in an afflicted loved one. It is a behavioral pattern in which the family shields the individual from experiencing the full impact or consequences of his behavior. This prevents the enabled person from being responsible and perpetuates his negative behavior and choices. The following are examples of enabling.

Faith in Action

A parent or spouse who chooses to care for a loved one who is unable to care for himself isn't just doing good work; they are doing God's work. Christ has called us all to care for the "least of these." The church should be a supportive community that offers the caregiver acceptance, assistance, comfort, and encouragement. No Christ follower should ever have to care for a mentally ill loved one alone.

SUGGESTED SCRIPTURES

Psalm 121:1–2	The Lord is our help in difficult times.
Matthew 6:34	Trust God and focus on today's issues.
Hebrew 6:10	God notices the care we provide to others.

BIBLICAL STORY TO CONNECT

Ruth and Naomi

Ruth 1:1–18	Being a caregiver requires sacrifice and great courage, but we can rest in the fact that God is in control of our futures.

- Keeping secrets about a loved one's behavior from others in order to avoid shame
- Ignoring a loved one's negative behavior
- Making excuses to others for a loved one's behavior
- Limiting the consequences of a loved one's behavior (e.g., paying his debts, fixing his tickets)
- Blaming others for a loved one's behavior

■ Altering the family's daily activities to keep the peace (e.g., avoiding the loved one)

■ Doing for the loved one what he should do for himself

It is important to understand that while behaviors and choices can be enabled, a mental illness cannot. For example, bipolar disorder is a mental illness, not a choice. You cannot enable a person to be more bipolar. Destructive behavior (e.g., substance abuse) or poor choices (e.g., excessive spending) by a person with bipolar disorder, however, can be enabled.

All family members who enable share one commonality—they love someone who is out of control. It is difficult to see a loved one suffer. Thus, to relieve suffering and make life more peaceful, an enabler takes responsibility for the loved one's poor choices. This allows the enabler to feel in control of an unmanageable situation. Enablers believe they are doing these things out of love, when actually they are doing them out of fear and shame. They think, "I have to fix this, so no one finds out" or "If I don't intervene, I may lose my son." But ultimately, the result of enabling is not peace and control, but guilt and pain.

The role of the pastoral counselor is to help family members recognize the areas where they have taken responsibility for their loved one's negative behavior and to guide them toward change. The goal is to move from enabling to empowering. Empowering means putting in place opportunities for a loved one to grow and succeed on his recovery journey. This involves setting healthy boundaries, building responsibility and purpose, and developing a structured plan to make daily life easier to manage.

Joan was at her wits end when she first met with Pam, a pastoral counselor at her church. One year before, her thirty-three-year-old son Richard had moved in with her. Diagnosed with schizophrenia at the age of twenty-three, Richard was never able to complete college due to his illness. After leaving college, he initially lived with his father but was no longer welcome there. Over the last ten years, he had bounced around between the homes of friends and girlfriends. He had been unable to hold any job for more than a few weeks and refused psychiatric treatment, believing his diagnosis was in error and that his problems in life were the result of external factors rather than mental illness. Unable to find a place to live, Richard had asked his mother if he could move in with her for a few weeks until he got back on his feet. While he aspired to a have a career in computers, he had never been able to make any progress toward that goal.

Joan described to Pam what the last year had been like living with Richard. He slept till noon most days and then obsessively watched the same set of television programs throughout the afternoon. He would eat dinner alone in his room before going out to a local bar. He would drink at the bar for several hours and then drive, intoxicated, back to the house. Most nights he would stay up till two or three in the morning playing video games. Joan said that her house was a mess. Richard never cleaned up after himself and constantly begged her for money, which he used for gas, cigarettes, and alcohol. If she asked him to do anything around the house, it would result in a fight, so she simply stopped asking. Joan told Pam that she also gave Richard money and paid for his cell phone to avoid conflict.

"I'm exhausted," Joan said. "I work all day and come home to a disaster. I'm concerned that he is going to hurt himself or someone else because of his drinking and driving. I love my son, but honestly I wish he would leave."

Pam explained to Joan that she had fallen into a pattern of enabling Richard's bad behavior. She suggested that they begin to meet weekly so that Joan could learn better ways to interact with Richard and begin to build a healthy mother-son relationship. Pam began by educating Joan on the symptoms of schizophrenia so that she could better understand what Richard was going through on a daily basis. Next they set up boundaries. Richard was not allowed to have alcohol in the home or to smoke in the house. He also would receive a set amount of money each week as an allowance. After that, they began to institute opportunities for Richard to be successful with small jobs around the house. At first, he was responsible for simply feeding the dog every day, but his responsibility ultimately grew to completing a list of tasks that Joan left for Richard—and to complete them before she got home from work. If Richard did not complete the tasks or respect the boundaries, he would not receive his weekly allowance. All of these changes were made slowly, over weeks and months. Richard was very resistant at first and acted out. He would become angry and attempt to shame or scare Joan into giving him what he wanted. But Pam helped Joan stay with the plan, and slowly, after a few weeks, they began to see positive change. After one year of working with Pam, Joan said that she and Richard's relationship was the best it had ever been. He was helpful around the home, respectful to her, and no longer drinking and driving. He was also seeing a psychiatrist for treatment. Joan was feeling better as well, and for the first time, she had real hope for her son's future.

PROBLEM-SOLVING

Problem-solving is often more difficult for the person in the middle of a troubling situation than for someone looking in from the outside. Because of the daily burden placed on caregivers, even manageable problems associated with their loved ones can become overwhelming and almost impossible to solve. As someone removed from the emotional weight of the situation, the pastoral counselor has the opportunity to help caregivers learn how to systematically break down problems so that they might more easily find solutions. Teach the caregiver to follow the problem-solving process below whenever a challenge presents itself.

- **Write Down the Problem**—It is often hard to pinpoint specific issues in an overwhelming situation. Writing down the specific problem helps you find a starting point.
- **Break the Problem Down into Smaller Issues**—Look at the problem and begin to break it down into the smaller issues that make up the larger overwhelming concern. This can help you begin to identify where many of the smaller issues arise.
- **Manage What You Can Control**—Many times, taking care of the few things you can control will help you manage the larger problem and bring stability to the situation.

- **Identify Solutions**—Write down possible solutions to the smaller issues you do not have control over. Ask trusted friends and family members to help you develop ideas.
- **Determine Necessary Roles**—You do not have to do this alone. Identify who the primary person working with your loved one on these issues will be and what other supportive roles are needed.
- **Pinpoint Potential Roadblocks**—Most plans don't work exactly as designed. Identify where the roadblocks may be and what solutions can be applied.

PASTORAL CARE AND THE FAMILY

Family caregivers play many roles in the care of their loved ones with mental illness. They provide them with day-to-day physical care, monitor their mental state (to identify early signs of relapse or decline), help them access services, supervise their medications, meet the family's financial needs, and provide emotional support. Due to the time and energy required of caregivers, their social and leisure activities are often limited. When combined with the discrimination and stigma associated with mental illness, this means caregivers are often isolated and alienated from their usual support networks. Over time, this can result in emotional exhaustion, depression, and burnout.[11] Thus, the pastoral counselor has a vital role in helping caregivers to maintain their spiritual and emotional health.

Faith. Caregivers who are believers often rely on their faith to cope with the stress. Religious beliefs and practices can provide a sense of hope, control, and psychological well-being.[12] Family members who rely on their faith to cope report better relationships with their afflicted loved ones and healthier self-care practices.[13] Prayer and seeking support and reassurance from God are the most frequently used religious coping strategies.

Unfortunately, not all religious coping mechanisms are beneficial to the caregiver. Negative religious coping strategies include being angry with God, believing God is punishing you or your loved one, and feeling abandoned by God.[14] Such negative responses have been shown to be harmful, only increasing the caregiver's despair and hopelessness. The pastoral counselor has the opportunity to help caregivers grow in their relationships with Christ by encouraging them to develop positive religious coping strategies and to avoid negative ones (see examples of each below). The knowledge that we serve a loving God who hears our desperate cries and responds with sustaining grace is truly life-changing.

Examples of Positive Religious Coping Strategies
- Seeking help from God for my problems
- Asking for spiritual guidance from religious leaders or fellow believers
- Pursuing a stronger connection with God
- Viewing circumstances as an opportunity for spiritual growth
- Asking for forgiveness of sin
- Using religious practices (e.g., prayer, Bible study) to minimize worry and stress

Examples of Negative Religious Coping Strategies
- Wondering if God has abandoned me
- Being convinced that God is punishing me and/or my loved one
- Questioning God's love and goodness
- Viewing my circumstances as the work of Satan or demons
- Doubting God's power
- Believing that my church or fellow believers have abandoned me

Grieving. Much like the death of a close friend or relative, serious mental illness in a loved one can cause a caregiver to grieve the passing of the person they once knew. Parents, in particular, have to readjust their expectations for the future when a child (even an adult child) develops a serious mental illness. In the process, they may need to grieve the hopes and dreams they once had for their child. As a pastoral counselor, it is important to help the counselee understand that grieving is a normal God-ordained process for emotional healing. Jesus himself had to take time to grieve after the death of his cousin John the Baptist (Matt. 14:12–21).

In addition, the pastoral counselor has the opportunity to walk with the family as they move through the five stages of the grieving process: denial, anger, bargaining, depression, and acceptance.[15] Problems that can hinder one's ability to successfully complete the grieving process include getting stuck and cycling. For example, a father may become stuck at the denial stage, unable to fully accept the inevitable consequences of what has happened to his child. The most common stage in which people become stuck is depression. Cycling occurs when a person moves forward without completing an earlier stage, causing them to cycle back and repeat a previous stage. Both of these problems will hinder a caregiver's ability to heal.

At the same time, the stages should not be understood as rigid stops on a linear timeline but, rather, as a processing framework. Not everyone goes through all of the stages or follows them in a set order. So it is useful to help the counselee identify the stage of grief she is presently experiencing and any progress she has made. Below are brief descriptions of each of the five stages.

- Stage 1: Denial—Trying to avoid the inevitable consequences or the future
- Stage 2: Anger—Feeling an explosive outpouring of bottled-up emotions
- Stage 3: Bargaining—Seeking ways to keep the inevitable from occurring
- Stage 4: Depression—Experiencing a deep-seated hopelessness for the future
- Stage 5: Acceptance—Being actively involved in moving on to the next phase of life

Show these stages and their descriptions to grieving individuals and ask them to identify which stages they feel they have completed and which stage they believe they are presently experiencing. This exercise can help counselees recognize whether they are stuck or cycling and how they might move forward in the grieving process.

Guilt. Caregivers often carry the additional emotional burden of overwhelming guilt.[16] This undeserved guilt occurs for a variety of reasons. Caregivers may believe that they aren't doing enough for their afflicted loved ones or that their caregiving is inadequate. Guilt may arise when they feel burdened by the caregiver role or wish for a break. Caregivers also can hold guilt for difficult treatment decisions they may have had to make, such as hospitalizing a loved one against her will, calling the police during a mental health crisis, or requiring a loved one to take psychiatric medications that have serious negative side effects.

Parents caring for a child with a mental illness frequently blame themselves for their child's disorder. They often ask, "What did I do wrong?" or "How could I have prevented this?" They hold the false belief that the disorder resulted from or was aggravated by something they did or did not do as parents, such as being too strict or too passive, not spending enough time with their child, not showing enough love and affection, or getting a divorce. This type of guilt-driven caregiving often leads to enabling behavior.

To help family members move beyond undeserved guilt, encourage them to recognize and internalize three basic truths of caregiving: First, their loved one's mental disorder is not their fault! Mental illnesses are medical conditions in the same way diabetes and cancer are. And while caregivers are not responsible for causing the disorder, there are a number of things they can do to minimize a loved one's suffering and facilitate the process of recovery (e.g., help them obtain mental health care, provide them with a daily structure and routine, educate themselves about the illness).

Second, there is no such thing as perfect caregiving. There will always be a difference between what they believe needs to be done (i.e., perfect caregiving) and what they're willing and able to do (i.e., reality). They must accept that difference as a fact of life and not a personal failure and then learn to live with it. They owe their afflicted loved ones nothing more than good-effort caregiving in love; perfect outcomes are simply impossible.

Finally, the role of caregiver is physically, mentally, and spiritually overwhelming for everyone. A caregiver is not weak if he feels burdened or wants to take a break; that is normal and expected. The caregiver's life did not stop when his loved one was diagnosed with a mental illness. If caregivers stop living for themselves, they will come to resent their loved ones, which will only bring greater feelings of guilt. Remind them that taking time to maintain their health is not selfish or neglectful but, rather, equips them to be better caregivers.

Support Groups. When surveyed, caregivers reported that education about mental illness (psychoeducation) and the use of support groups were the two strategies that most improved their ability to cope.[17] Psychoeducational support groups provide caregivers with education and information about mental illness along with opportunities to receive support and ministry from others in the group. These groups have been shown to reduce social isolation, to increase social support, and—when they are faith-based—to enhance spiritual growth.[18] In addition, participation in a psychoeducational support group has been shown to secondarily benefit the caregiver's afflicted love one, reducing rehospitalizations and lessening the severity of symptoms.[19] Faith communities are well positioned to provide psychoeducational groups for isolated caregivers who are desperately in need of human connection and support. A number of organizations have developed faith-based caregiver support-group curricula and training, which are available to churches. These organizations include Fresh Hope (https://freshhope.us/), Grace Alliance (https://mentalhealthgracealliance.org/), and the Hope and Healing Center & Institute (https://mentalhealthgateway.org/).

Communication

You may remember the old adage "Sticks and stones may break my bones, but words will never hurt me." What a lie! Words do hurt. In fact, the scriptures tell us that the tongue is like a fire (James 3:6), with the power of life and death in it (Prov. 18:21). Words are powerful. They can be used to bring healing to the hurting, or they can be weaponized to cause deep, long-lasting pain. Proverbs provides the pastoral counselor with a helpful guide for using godly communication: listen before you speak (18:13), consider your words (12:18), don't talk too much (17:27), speak the truth (12:22), and use your words to build others up (15:14). When a pastoral counselor chooses to communicate in this way, those in distress will find her words to be "like apples of gold in settings of silver" (Prov. 25:11).

STARTING THE CONVERSATION

While a majority of those living with serious mental illness and their family members believe that churches should talk more openly about mental illness, more than 60 percent of Protestant pastors report rarely or never speaking about the topic in sermons or large group meetings.[1] Sadly, only 12 percent of church leaders feel that mental illness is openly discussed in a healthy way within their congregations.[2]

As a pastoral counselor, you have the opportunity to help your church's clergy and ministry staff develop a safe and accepting environment for those living with serious mental illness. Below are suggestions for simple changes you can promote that will help start a conversation about mental illness within your faith community.

- Pray collectively during the service each week for those who are struggling with a mental disorder. Use the actual names of the disorders during the prayer (e.g., depression, schizophrenia, bipolar disorder).
- Prepare sermons that acknowledge the struggles experienced by those living with mental illness and their families.
- Invite a member of the church who has struggled with mental illness to share his testimony with the congregation.
- Place brochures and other sources of information regarding mental illness and available mental health resources in the back of the church, in the bulletin, or in the pews.
- Invite mental health professionals to speak or offer seminars on topics like suicide or addiction at the church.

While a senior pastor or elder board may initially be resistant to some of these suggestions, they are unlikely to refuse all of them. Do what you can. It's all about starting a conversation. Experience shows us that once a conversation starts, most pastors and churches become receptive to changes.

USING LIFE-GIVING WORDS

One way to eliminate the stigma related to mental illness is to carefully choose our words when describing mental health conditions and the people who live with them. We can choose to speak words that give life or words that shame.

Stigmatizing language brings shame. Its purpose is to minimize, disgrace, or dehumanize someone in order to justify inaction and lack of compassion. Derogatory terms such as "crazy," "nuts," "psycho," and "loony" constitute stigmatizing language and have unfortunately become part of everyday lingo.[3] These terms express contempt and disrespect toward individuals living with mental illness, even if the words are not being spoken directly to them; they simply should not be used. Using mental health terms to explain everyday individual quirks or behaviors that are common to many—for example, using "OCD" to describe someone who is organized or "anorexic" to depict a woman who is thin—is also stigmatizing. Such mental health clichés minimize the severity of mental disorders and further confuse people's limited understanding of these complex conditions.

When speaking of those who have been legitimately diagnosed with mental health conditions, always put the person first, not the illness. For instance, do not use language that defines people according to their diagnoses, such as, "He's schizophrenic" or "She is a bipolar." A person is far more than a diagnosis. Instead say, "He has been diagnosed with schizophrenia" or "She is living with bipolar disorder." Likewise, when talking about a suicide, do not say that a person "committed suicide." The word "committed" suggests that the individual performed a reasoned and rational act, much like if someone has "committed a crime" or "committed a sin." Rather, say that the individual "died by suicide." In situations in which it was commonly known that the person was struggling with a diagnosed mental disorder, it may also be appropriate to say that the death resulted from the disorder. For example, "he died as a result of depression" or "her death was the result of bipolar disorder."

As a pastoral counselor, you can help educate your congregation and ministry staff in the best language to use when talking about mental illness.

ACTIVE LISTENING

Listening is perhaps the most important communication skill you can develop to enhance the effectiveness of your pastoral counseling ministry. While it is not uncommon to be more focused on what you are going to say next than on what the speaker is currently saying, this listening approach is simply not useful within the counseling environment. The goal of listening, for the pastoral counselor, should be to fully understand the distressed individual's situation while offering support and empathy. This approach is referred to as active listening.[4] Active listening makes the speaker feel heard and valued. The following are tips to help you improve your active listening skills.

Pay Attention. Silence all technology and move away from any external distractions. Quiet your internal dialogue. It is impossible to actively listen to someone else and your own inner voice at the same time. Focus on what is being said rather than on what you want to say. Do not be preparing your reply while the other person is speaking. If you are truly paying attention, you should be able to accurately repeat the speaker's last sentence.

Be Aware of Nonverbal Behavior. "Listen" to the speaker's tone of voice and body language to pick up on unspoken emotions and hidden meanings. Nonverbal behaviors, such as facial expressions, can often tell you more than words.

Demonstrate That You Are Listening. Make eye contact while the other person is speaking. Use body language and gestures to show that you are engaged. Lean in toward the other person, keeping your posture open and inviting. Avoid folding your arms, as this signals that you are not listening. Nod occasionally and encourage the speaker to continue by making small verbal comments such as "yes" and "uh-huh."

Paraphrase. Rather than offering advice or opinions, reflect back what has been said. You might start this off by saying, "What I'm hearing is . . ." or "In other words, what you are saying is . . ." Restating key points you have heard and asking whether they are accurate is an easy way to avoid misunderstanding and clarify any confusion.

Be Okay with Silence. Allow moments of silence to resolve naturally. You don't always have to reply or make a comment to keep the dialogue going. A break in the conversation can give everyone an opportunity to collect their thoughts.

Show Interest by Asking Questions. Open-ended questions (e.g., "What do you think about . . . ?" or "Tell me about . . .") are an important part of active listening. They encourage self-reflection and problem-solving. Closed (yes-or-no) questions, on the other hand, tend to shut down the conversation, so avoid these. Always allow the speaker to finish a point before asking a question.

VALIDATE—AFFIRM—RECONCILE

When an individual is struggling with severe psychological distress, his ability to effectively process information is altered. This disruption of thought can result in confusion, poor self-awareness, and the misinterpretation of words and actions. In this state, the person is more likely to react from emotion than respond out of reason, making communication difficult and extremely frustrating. Trying to correct or logically convince the person of your point will likely increase his agitation and escalate the situation. A better approach for communicating with those in distress is to connect with them emotionally using the Validate-Affirm-Reconcile method described below.

Validate. Instead of focusing on the accuracy of the words they are saying, determine the specific emotions they are feeling (e.g., fear, sadness). Appeal to their hearts with love rather than to their minds with reason. Reflect their feelings back to them and validate the emotions they are experiencing (e.g., "I can see that you are frightened, and I appreciate why you are feeling that way"). It is not important that you agree with their words or feelings, but only that you validate their emotional experience.

Affirm. To counter the feelings of isolation and rejection that the person may be experiencing, affirm the individual as a person of faith in Christ and as a valued friend, family member, or congregant (e.g., "God cares about what you are going through. You are important to me, and I want to help you get through this"). Reassuring people that they are cared for and loved despite their present circumstances will promote a sense of acceptance and emotional safety.

Reconcile. Offer the person an opportunity for reconciliation by providing the grace necessary to find a point of common ground (e.g., "I know we don't have all the answers right now, but I will walk through this with you and we can find the answers together along the way"). Suggest practical solutions that might give the individual opportunities to improve her present situation. The goal is to build hope and restore harmony to the relationship.

DE-ESCALATION

Given the wide variety of people that interact on a church campus, it is likely that some will become agitated, angry, and argumentative. Pastoral counselors are often called in to diffuse these challenging situations. The following is a four-step process for de-escalation that can keep this type of interaction from becoming a crisis: assess the situation, maintain control, actively listen, and engage.[5]

Assess the Situation. Ask questions about the scenario to determine the current level of escalation and the potential for physical danger so that you can respond appropriately. *Is the individual armed or being physically violent?* If so, immediately leave the area and call the police. *What are your physical surroundings?* If you are in a confined space, like a small office, move to a larger open area. Place yourself in a position to easily exit. Prevent cornering yourself or the other person, and allow the individual space to move around. Do not touch the person, even if you know each other, as this may be interpreted as a threatening gesture, which could elicit an aggressive response. Move away from any objects or furniture that could be easily picked up and thrown. If possible, make others aware of the situation. *Do you know this person?* A person's name is the most meaningful word in his vocabulary. Saying a person's name immediately focuses his attention. *Do you know why this person is at the church?* This information will be useful during your interaction.

Maintain Control. How you respond in an escalated situation will determine who is in charge of the interaction. To successfully de-escalate, you must be in control. So do not panic or act too quickly. Do not ask for permission for your actions (e.g., "Would it be okay if I . . . ?"). Remove spectators and triggering persons from the area. And slow things down. Assume a relaxed body posture and speak in a normal voice. Model the type of interaction you would like to see from the individual. Being loud and threatening does not make one in charge.

Practice Active Listening. Pay full attention to the person's story using active listening. Don't change the subject or interrupt. Giving people the chance to say what they need to say will help calm their escalating emotions.

Engage. Using the Validate-Affirm-Reconcile method, engage the person. Address the individual by name. If you do not know her name, ask. Do not tell the person to "calm down." While it may seem like an obvious thing to say, it is ineffective when addressing a person who is having an emotional crisis. Recognize any hesitation in the person's speech, and use these opportunities to interject or make suggestions.

CASE EXAMPLES

The following examples are based on actual church encounters and demonstrate how the communication skills presented above might be used to effectively de-escalate an emotionally charged situation.

CASE EXAMPLE 1. A young man in his late twenties has come to the church looking for help in paying his electric bill. The first person he encounters is Jennifer, a receptionist, who informs him that the church does not offer direct financial aid but refers people to a nearby Christian social-service organization that provides such assistance. The man becomes angry and starts yelling at Jennifer. You hear the yelling from your office, and you get up to check on the situation.

Assess the Situation. As you enter the reception area, you see the young man, red-faced, leaning over the reception desk and yelling at Jennifer. You do not recognize him. He is wearing jeans and a T-shirt. In his hand is what appears to be a utility bill, which he is waving around in the air. He does not appear to be armed. His posture is aggressive, and Jennifer appears frightened. You, Jennifer, and the young man are the only people in the small reception area.

Resolving Conflict

The scriptures provide clear instructions on how we are to communicate with one another. As James writes, we are to "be quick to hear, slow to speak, and slow to anger." The apostle Paul adds that our conversations should be "full of grace." In times of conflict, we must allow the indwelling Holy Spirit to calm our emotions and give us the eyes of Christ for those in distress.

SUGGESTED SCRIPTURES

Proverbs 15:1   How we speak affects how others respond to us.

Galatians 6:1   God has called us to help restore those who have sinned.

Colossians 3:13   A heart of forgiveness is necessary for resolving conflict.

BIBLICAL STORY TO CONNECT

Jesus and Legion

Luke 8:26–33   Successfully engaging a person in distress requires meeting the person where they are emotionally, not where you want them to be.

Maintain Control. You quietly ask Jennifer to exit the reception area, leaving you and the young man alone. You position yourself away from the desk in a more open area of the room. In a normal, calm voice, you ask him his name. He angrily replies, "Rob." You introduce yourself and say that you are here to help. You then ask him to tell you what is going on.

Practice Active Listening. In a profanity-laced tirade, focused mostly on Jennifer and Christianity, he explains that this is the third church today that he has gone to for help, with no success. This is his second missed bill payment, and his power will likely be turned off any day now. He recently lost his job, and he has a young child at home who is ill. It becomes clear to you that his anger is driven by the frustration and shame of not being able to provide for his family as well as fear for his ill child.

Engage. You wait for hesitation in Rob's speech before engaging him. "Rob, I can hear the anger and frustration in your voice. I would feel the same if my child was home ill and the power was about to be shut off. Rob, I'm so glad that God has led you here, so we can help you. You and your family are important to us. I'm going to go sit on that bench out-side and call a friend of mine at the organization Jennifer mentioned to get you help with your electric bill. Rob, why don't you come outside with me." Rob follows you outside. You sit on the bench and call someone at the Christian social-service organization. You explain the situation on the phone, ask what assistance can be provided, and let them know that Rob is on his way over. You explain to Rob what to expect, provide him with the name of the person you spoke with on the phone, and give him directions to the organization. You give him your business card and tell him to call you if he has any problems.

CASE EXAMPLE 2. A man began attending services at your church several weeks ago. Each Sunday, he shows up with his clothing disheveled and look-ing very upset. Today he is sitting in the back pew, when suddenly, in the middle of the service, he stands up and starts pacing. He is visibly agitated and starts muttering things about God and the devil to the people around him. At this point, people around the sanctuary begin to take notice, which agitates him even further. He begins talking loudly, pointing at people, and accusing them of being evil.

Assess the Situation. As you approach the man, you recognize him from previous Sundays but do not know his name. He is approximately thirty-five and is wearing a wrinkled suit that is several sizes too big. He does not appear to be armed. He is pacing back and forth along the back aisle of the church. There are several hundred people in the sanctuary, but he does not appear to be shouting at any specific person—just at those in his general area. The pastor, recognizing the disruption, has asked the worship team to return to the stage and to lead the congregation in several songs. Some of the ushers are trying to move the man out of the sanctuary. He loudly refuses to leave and appears to be growing more agitated. Your instinct may be to try and quiet or move the man, so that the service will not be disrupted, but you must suppress that thought. This man is in distress. He is spiritually confused and has been drawn to the church. The relief of his suffering is more important to God than the service. This is a divine opportunity to teach the congregation about true grace.

Maintain Control. You ask the ushers to move away. (In many churches, it is not uncommon for off-duty police officers to provide security on Sunday mornings. But this situation has not risen to the level of a criminal offense as of yet. So if an officer is present, ask him to give you an opportunity to de-escalate the situation. My personal opinion is that individuals in distress should only be physically removed from a church service against their will if they are being violent or threatening others with physical harm.) In a normal, calm voice, you introduce yourself and ask him his name. He loudly says that only the name of Jesus matters. You respond, "That is so true. Here, we believe that Jesus is the name above all names. I'm glad you have joined us today. Tell me what is upsetting you right now."

Practice Active Listening. He begins to incoherently describe a broad range of unrelated topics, ranging from his fear of the demonic taking over his mind to his belief that the federal government is trying to stop him from speaking the truth about Jesus. It is clear that he is deeply fearful and not self-aware. You ask if he lives near the church, and he says that he lives in a nearby group home.

Engage. You ask him his name, and he says, "Tim." You say, "Tim, we are so glad that you came to worship with us today. You seem to have a lot of questions about God and faith, and I really appreciate your honesty. I would love to talk more with you about this, but it is hard for me to hear you in here. Let's go out in the lobby where it will be easier for me to hear you." You turn to leave the sanctuary and Tim follows. In the lobby, you find out that he was raised a Christian and has long struggled with mental health problems. He lives at a nearby group home but has not been taking his medication recently, because he fears it is poison. You tell him, "Tim, the way you have held onto your faith through very difficult times is inspiring. We are so blessed that you have decided to be part of our fellowship. Can I pray for you?" After you pray, you give him a new Bible and your business card. "Tim, if you ever want to talk about God again, just give me a call. Would you let me call your home so that someone could come and pick you up?" He agrees.

> **While no two situations** will ever be the same and it is impossible to predict how any given individual will react, these de-escalation steps have been shown to be helpful with those in emotional crisis. Always remember that communication, for the pastoral counselor, is less about using reason and eloquent words and far more about having patience and a heart of grace.

Restoration

Mental Health
Ministries

O n February 17, 2011, antigovernment protest in the Libyan
city of Benghazi erupted into a violent national rebellion against the
authoritarian dictator Colonel Muammar al-Qaddafi. In the nine-month
civil war that followed, it is estimated that 30,000 Libyans were killed and
50,000 injured. In April 2011, representatives of the new transitional government contacted Acts of Mercy International (AMI), a United States–
based Christian relief and development organization, to inquire if they
could send experts to advise them on how to begin rebuilding the long
neglected Libyan educational system. In October 2011, I was asked to
be part of the team of educators that traveled to Benghazi. By the time
we arrived in Libya, however, priorities had changed, and mental health
issues—specifically trauma—were now the predominant problem.

What we found in Benghazi was a highly traumatized civilian population adversely affected by both the ongoing civil war and years of oppres-
sion under a tyrannical regime (i.e., systematic rape, political imprisonment,
torture). Post-traumatic stress disorder (PTSD) was common among civil-
ians and combatants alike. Children were showing signs of trauma-induced

regression (i.e., losing previously acquired skills and abilities): wetting the bed, clinging to their parents, and no longer able to talk. The civil war had also displaced tens of thousands, who were now living in harsh conditions at IDP (indigenous displaced person) camps throughout the region. It was apparent, however, that the Libyan mental health system was inadequate and unable to deal with these significant psychiatric and psychological problems.

Over the next two years, I was privileged to co-lead an effort with AMI to provide trauma-informed care to eastern Libya. To begin, we developed a ten-week curriculum for a psychosocial trauma group for adults and a six-week art therapy intervention for traumatized children aged three to twelve. The materials we developed were translated into Arabic, and we chose a name for the trauma groups: *shifa*, which, in Arabic, means "healing." At the time, Libya, a country of 6.3 million people, had fewer than thirty psychiatrists and no licensed psychologists or social workers, so we trained laymen to lead the shifa groups. In addition, we provided intensive training in trauma-informed psychological care to physicians and nurses in hospitals throughout the region.

The results of those two years of intervention were nothing short of miraculous. Every day we saw men, women, and children healed from the deep wounds of trauma.[1] And perhaps more important, we were able to share the love of Christ with hurting people who had long been thought to be unreachable. Since that time, the trauma group resources we developed during our time in Libya have been used to help other traumatized individuals both in the United States and abroad, including refugees of the Syrian civil war, child soldiers in Somalia, combat veterans, and victims of domestic violence and sexual assault.

My time in Libya taught me that mental health ministry can open doors for the gospel that more traditional ministry approaches cannot. As such, in churches that offer ministries for prison inmates, veterans, or those suffering from addiction, homelessness, domestic violence, or natural disasters, the greater focus on mental health increases opportunities for sharing Jesus with those in distress.

THE CHURCH AND MENTAL HEALTH CARE

Since its beginning, the church has been involved in caring for the "least of these." Jesus called us to serve him by being his hands and feet to the poor, orphaned, widowed, homeless, and sick (Matt. 25:35–40). Today most churches meet this call through a variety of ministries, including programs for those who are addicted, incarcerated, homeless, sex-trafficked, traumatized, and abused. All of these hurting individuals share a common characteristic: severe psychological distress. In fact, research finds that mental health problems occur in these groups at significantly higher rates than in the general population.[2] It could be said, then, that because of these ministries to the psychologically distressed, churches are already involved in mental health care; they just don't realize it. Unfortunately, because few ministries recognize, let alone take into account, the mental health difficulties of the individuals they are serving, they often focus solely on their spiritual needs.

My friend and colleague Dr. Eric Johnson, director of the Gideon Institute of Christian Psychology and Counseling at Houston Baptist University, uses the term "biblically rooted and clinically informed" to describe mental health care practiced from a Christian worldview. This term can also be used to guide our mental health–related ministries within the local church. A ministry that is "biblically rooted and clinically informed" is one that is carried out through the application of both biblical truth and psychological science. It relieves physical and psychological suffering in those with mental health problems while revealing the unconditional love and limitless grace that is available only through a personal relationship with Jesus Christ.

ADDICTION MINISTRIES

While most people think of addiction as a physiological or psychological dependence on alcohol or drugs, research suggests that any act or behavior capable of stimulating the reward centers of the brain may become addictive. Therefore, addiction can be more broadly defined as a compulsive drive to use an intoxicating substance (i.e., substance addiction) or to perform a specific reinforcing act or behavior (i.e., behavioral addiction), despite knowledge of its personal negative consequences. Common addiction ministries include those related to alcohol and drugs, hypersexuality, overeating, and gambling.

Alcohol and Drugs. The characteristic symptom of a substance addiction is a compulsive pattern of alcohol or drug use that leads to significant impairment or distress in the individual's life. An estimated 7.6 percent of adults (19 million individuals) meet criteria for a substance addiction in a given year. Substance addiction is referred to as "substance use disorder" in the *DSM-5*. Individuals with substance addictions show higher rates of anxiety disorders, mood disorders, and personality disorders than the general population. Substance addictions are more common among men than women.[3]

Hypersexuality. A sex addiction is characterized by an abnormal, intense, and obsessive drive for sex and/or sexual activities. While there are several types of sex addiction, churches tend to focus their ministry efforts on those involved in extreme promiscuity or the compulsive use of pornography. It is estimated that 5 percent of the adult population (13 million individuals) struggle with a sex addiction. Rates of depression and substance addiction are significantly higher in individuals with a sex addiction. In addition, sex addictions are four times more common in men than women.[4]

Overeating. A food addiction is characterized by compulsive, excessive, and dysregulated consumption of highly palatable, high-calorie foods (i.e., foods high in sugar, fat, and salt). It is estimated that 11 percent of the adult population (28 million individuals) suffer with a food addiction. Individuals with food addiction are usually obese or overweight. There is a significant overlap between the characteristic symptoms of binge-eating disorder as described in the *DSM-5* and food addiction. Individuals with food addiction are at an increased risk for depression, and food addiction is twice as prevalent among women as men.[5]

Gambling. A gambling addiction is characterized by repeated problematic gambling behavior that causes significant problems or distress for the individual. Gambling addiction is referred to as "gambling disorder" in the *DSM-5*. Online betting and fantasy sports have made it easier than ever to gamble. Approximately 1 percent of the adult population (2.5 million individuals) have a severe gambling problem. Individuals with gambling addictions show higher rates of substance addiction, depression, anxiety disorders, and personality disorders. Men develop gambling addictions at higher rates than women.[6]

Regardless of the type of addiction, a clinically informed addiction ministry recognizes that relapse is a common part of recovery and that addictions often co-occur with other mental disorders. Research finds that a vast majority (70 to 90 percent) of people in addiction recovery have at least one relapse before they're able to remain "sober" for any extended period of time. The majority of relapses occur within the first ninety days of abstinence.[7] It is important to understand that a relapse does not necessarily negate all the progress an individual has made up to that point. Especially if the relapse is a short-lived mistake, followed by an immediate return to the recovery process, that person should be encouraged about her progress. Recovery is a learning process, and sometimes people discover through relapse what they need to be aware of to successfully navigate life "sober." Research also finds that recovering addicts will generally be less likely to relapse as they accrue more and more "sober" time.

In the face of relapse, the pastoral counselor's response should be one of grace and mercy rather than of judgment and condemnation. Encourage those who relapse to forgive themselves and quickly return to the recovery process.

"Dual diagnosis" is the clinical term used to describe an individual who experiences a mental illness (e.g., depression) and an addiction at the same time. In these individuals, addiction is often an attempt to minimize the negative symptoms of the underlying mental disorder through "self-medication." *It is important to be aware that the presence of a co-occurring mental disorder in an addicted individual is associated with a higher rate of relapse following treatment.* Further, research has shown that it is more effective to treat co-occurring addictions and mental disorders together rather than separately.[8] That means those ministering to the addicted should receive training in how to recognize the signs and symptoms of mental illness. Mental Health First Aid (www.mentalhealthfirstaid.org) and Gateway to Hope (www.mentalhealthgateway.org) are two easily accessible options for mental health training. It also means that, if possible, all participants in an addiction ministry should be encouraged to obtain an evaluation to determine if they have any underlying mental health problems and, if so, to receive treatment. This type of evaluation is often available for low or no cost from a university's clinical psychology graduate program or from mental health-care providers in private practices who are willing to see a client or two each month *pro bono.*

JAIL AND PRISON MINISTRIES

The United States has the largest prison population in the world, exceeding both China and Russia. It is estimated that 2.2 million adults are held in American prisons and jails.[9] Sadly, mental illness is far more prevalent among the incarcerated than among the general population. The Bureau of Justice Statistics estimates that 56 percent of state prisoners, 45 percent of federal prisoners, and 64 percent of jail inmates suffer with a mental health problem. Within the juvenile justice system, 70 percent of incarcerated youth have at least one mental health condition. As such, jails and prisons have become our de facto mental asylums. In fact, in forty-four states, a jail or prison in the state holds more mentally ill individuals than the largest state psychiatric hospital.[10]

Churches tend to focus their ministry efforts on the evangelism of incarcerated individuals or on the assimilation of recently released inmates back into society. A clinically informed jail and prison ministry understands that a majority of inmates struggle with mental health problems. Those who evangelize within the walls of the jail or prison should receive training in how to recognize the signs and symptoms of mental illness, and if an inmate appears to be struggling with a mental health problem, the ministry provider should encourage him to seek assistance from the facility's mental health staff.

Ministries that work with recently released inmates should provide opportunities for them to be evaluated by a local mental health-care provider as part of their assimilation. As mentioned before, this type of evaluation is often available for low or no cost from a university's clinical psychology graduate program. Develop a comprehensive referral network for these individuals, and be prepared to cover the cost of any necessary mental health treatment for six to eight months.

HOMELESS MINISTRIES

The U.S. Department of Housing and Urban Development in the *2019 Annual Homeless Assessment Report to Congress* estimated that on a single night in January 2019, 568,000 people in the country experienced homelessness. Slightly more than two-thirds (63 percent) of those individuals were staying in sheltered locations, while just over one-third (37 percent) were in unsheltered locations. Approximately 100,000 of those individuals showed chronic patterns of homelessness. Of the chronically homeless, two-thirds were staying outdoors in abandoned buildings or other locations unsuitable for human habitation. Much as it is in the prison population, mental illness is prevalent among the chronically homeless. Research finds that 30 to 50 percent of homeless adults suffer with a serious mental illness, while 50 to 80 percent have a history of substance addiction. A clinically informed homeless ministry recognizes that mental illness and substance addiction are significant contributing factors in homelessness. As such, all ministry volunteers and staff working directly with the homeless should receive training on how to recognize the signs and symptoms of mental illness and addiction. Training in how to effectively communicate with those in distress and in crisis intervention techniques is also extremely helpful. Finally, homeless ministries should actively partner with local social-service organizations that offer mental health care for indigent clients, so that those who have been recognized as struggling with mental illness can be easily connected to professional care.

TRAUMA-RELATED MINISTRIES

Research finds that a majority of adults in the United States—61 percent of men and 51 percent of women—report exposure to at least one lifetime traumatic event; however, only a small percentage of individuals exposed to trauma go on to display a trauma-related disorder. Post-traumatic stress disorder (PTSD) is characterized by significant psychological distress (e.g., persistent frightening thoughts and memories) that lasts more than a month after one's exposure to a traumatic event that is potentially life-threatening (or perceived as life-threatening).[11] Psychologist Diane Langberg describes PTSD this way: "The memories of trauma infect victims' sleep, destroy their relationships and capacity to work, and torment their emotions. The wounds of trauma are not visible; the effects are."[12] In some sense, the person becomes trapped in the traumatic experience and is unable to move forward. PTSD occurs more frequently in women than in men. Common trauma-related ministries include those that serve survivors of natural disasters, sex trafficking, domestic violence, and combat. A greater emphasis on trauma-related mental health problems within these ministries would likely increase their success and broaden their impact.

Natural Disasters. Every year natural disasters kill an estimated 90,000 individuals and affect 160 million worldwide. Natural disasters include earthquakes, tsunamis, volcanic eruptions, landslides, hurricanes, tornados, floods, wildfires, and droughts. Research finds that 20 to 40 percent of survivors will develop PTSD following a natural disaster.[13] Many churches send relief teams into disaster areas (e.g., Haiti earthquake) to assist survivors with physical needs (e.g., food, water, shelter) and provide spiritual support.

Sex Trafficking. The Victims of Trafficking and Violence Protection Act of 2000 passed into law by the U.S. Congress and signed by President Clinton defines sex trafficking as "the recruitment, harboring, transportation, provision, or obtaining of a person for the purpose of a commercial sex act in which the commercial sex act is induced by force, fraud, or coercion, or in which the person forced to perform such an act is younger than age eighteen."[14] Types of sex trafficking include prostitution, pornography, stripping, live-sex shows, mail-order brides, military prostitution, and sex tourism. It is estimated that 15,000 to 50,000 women and children are trafficked annually for sexual exploitation in the United States.[15] Children in foster care, homeless youth, undocumented immigrant children, and those with substance abuse problems are especially at risk of being exploited. Given the physical and psychological abuse these women and children endure, it is not surprising that they suffer with significantly higher rates of substance addiction, anxiety, depression, and PTSD.[16] Sex-trafficking ministries typically seek to engage victims with the gospel, rescue them from exploitation, and provide them with an opportunity for healing and restoration.

Domestic Violence. The U.S. Department of Justice defines intimate partner violence, also called domestic violence, as a pattern of abusive behavior in any relationship, where that behavior is used by one intimate partner to gain or maintain power and control over another intimate partner. Intimate partner violence can include physical, sexual, and psychological abuse as well as economic coercion. The Centers for Disease Control and Prevention (CDC) estimate that one in three women in the United States will experience rape, physical violence, and/or stalking by an intimate partner in her lifetime; however, abuse and victimization by intimate partners is thought to be highly underreported.[17] Mental health problems such as depression, substance addiction, anxiety, and PTSD are common among victims of intimate partner violence.[18] Domestic violence ministries usually offer pastoral counseling and support groups for victims.

Combat Veterans. The first description of what we today call PTSD is attributed to Swiss military physicians who, in 1678, identified a pattern of physical and psychological symptoms caused by exposure to combat. This condition was characterized by melancholy (depression), incessant thoughts about home, disturbed sleep, weakness, loss of appetite, anxiety, cardiac palpitations, stupor, and fever. Clinical studies of U.S. combat veterans find PTSD prevalence rates of 12 percent in Vietnam veterans, 12 percent in Gulf War veterans, and 14 percent in veterans of Operation Enduring Freedom/Operation Iraqi Freedom. These rates are roughly four times that found in the general population (3.5 percent).[19] Veterans with PTSD also have higher rates of depression, substance addiction, domestic violence, and suicidality than the general populace. Ministries for combat veterans usually offer pastoral counseling and support groups for those with PTSD.

A clinically informed trauma-related ministry recognizes that trauma physically alters the victim's brain and that recovery is a long and painful process. Ministry staff and volunteers working with trauma victims should be equipped to recognize the symptoms of PTSD—intrusive thoughts (e.g., unwanted memories, nightmares), mood alterations (e.g., depression, shame, guilt), hypervigilance (e.g., an exaggerated startle response), and avoidance of all stimuli related to sensory and emotional trauma)—so that they can connect victims to professional caregivers if needed. They should also be trained in suicide prevention and trauma-focused psychological debriefing[20] so that they can offer immediate mental health support in the aftermath of trauma. This type of training is available through the American Association of Christian Counselors at https://www.lightuniversity.com /mentalhealthcoach/.

SMALL ACTS OF GRACE

While there are wonderful mental health resources and training available, your church may be very small, understaffed, or overwhelmed. Please know that a smile, an encouraging word, and a listening ear are powerful tools in helping those suffering with mental illness take the first step toward healing and recovery. Jesus calls believers to meet the basic needs of those in distress: "For I was hungry and you gave me something to eat, I was thirsty and you gave me something to drink, I was a stranger and you invited me in, I needed clothes and you clothed me, I was sick and you looked after me, I was in prison and you came to visit me" (Matt. 25:35–36). Small acts of grace matter, and God will powerfully use them.

Successful Mental Health Ministries

As validated by seven decades of research, the local church is the first place people go for help in addressing mental health problems.[1] While a majority of pastors and congregants believe that the church has a responsibility to provide resources and support for those living with serious mental illness, research finds that less than a quarter of churches offer any type of organized support for these individuals and their families.[2] On the other hand, some churches have fully embraced this divine opportunity and developed mental health ministries that are transforming lives and restoring hope. The following successful mental health ministries demonstrate how churches of varying sizes are engaging the crisis and serving those affected by serious mental illness.

Saddleback Church (Lake Forest Campus)

Average Weekend Worship Attendance: 11,500–12,000
Location: Lake Forest, CA (county population of 3.2 million)
Setting: Suburban

Denomination: Southern Baptist

Website: www.saddleback.com

History: Ministering to those with mental health problems has always been an important part of pastoral care at Saddleback Church. Early on, the church developed a biblically based church counselor training program. This training prepares congregants to become part of the church's lay counseling ministry. Volunteers receive extensive training, ongoing supervision, and continuing education. The church has also long offered a variety of support groups at several of its campuses. For example, Celebrate Recovery (www.celebraterecovery.com), arguably the most successful faith-based recovery group in the world, was originally developed at Saddleback and remains an important part of the church's care ministry. The commitment of Saddleback Church to people living with mental illness greatly increased in 2013 following the suicide of Pastor Rick and Kay Warren's youngest son. Out of this tragedy, Saddleback's Hope for Mental Health Ministry (www .hope4mentalhealth.com) was born.

Staffing: Two full-time staff and thirty lay volunteers

Partnerships: The Hope for Mental Health Ministry has formed partnerships with the National Alliance on Mental Illness (www.nami.org) and the American Foundation for Suicide Prevention (www.afsp.org).

Mission: Extend the radical friendship of Jesus to individuals living with mental illness and their families by providing transforming love, support, and hope through the local church.

Mental Health Services: The Hope for Mental Health Ministry hosts a monthly gathering called the Hope for Mental Health Community. This gathering "is a safe place for anyone living with mental illness, family members, friends, and anyone who has a passion to journey with others toward hope."[3] The monthly meeting includes a devotional, an invited speaker, a question-and-answer session, and a time for fellowship and prayer. Attendees can participate in the gathering in person or through FaceTime live. The Hope for Mental Health Ministry also offers a three-day REACH training event for staff and lay leaders from churches across the country. There, they learn best practices for launching and building mental health ministries in their faith communities.

First Corinthian Baptist Church

Average Weekend Worship Attendance: 6,500–7,000
Location: Harlem, NY (county population 8.4 million)
Setting: Urban
Denomination: American Baptist
Website: www.fcbcnyc.org
History: The HOPE (Healing On Purpose and Evolving) Center is the fulfillment of First Corinthian's senior pastor's vision to effectively support the vast array of mental health needs in the Harlem community. Opened in December 2016, the center seeks to minimize the stigma associated with mental health services that presently exists in communities of color. It is the first faith-based mental health facility in Harlem.
Staffing: Four full-time employees and four graduate clinical interns
Partnerships: The HOPE Center has established partnerships with a wide variety of hospitals, professional organizations, academic institutions, and nonprofit organizations. These include Harlem Hospital, Northwell Health, Buddhist Insights (www.buddhistinsights.com), Hunter College, Columbia University, the New York State Psychiatric Institute (www.nyspi.org), the New York Academy of Medicine (www.nyam.org), the National Urban League (www.nul.org), and Presbyterian Senior Services (www.pssusa.org).
Mission: To provide quality therapeutic services in Harlem wherever mental health-care barriers exist.
Mental Health Services: The HOPE Center offers therapy for individuals, couples, and families. Clients are given ten free clinical sessions before being referred to a mental health-care provider in the community. In addition, the center offers a variety of weekly support services and

self-help groups, including grief support, a mindfulness moment (an opportunity to calm one's thoughts and focus attention on the present moment), men's empowerment, women's empowerment, relapse prevention, and help for religious trauma.

St. Martin's Episcopal Church

Average Weekend Worship Attendance: 2,300–2,400

Location: Houston, TX (county population 4.7 million)

Setting: Suburban

Denomination: Episcopal

Website: www.stmartinsepiscopal.org

History: Following a parish-wide survey conducted in the early 2000s and subsequent study and inquiry by the vestry and rector, the members of St. Martin's committed to be more intentional in their outreach to those hurting throughout the community. Established in 2011, the Hope and Healing Center & Institute (HHCI; www .hopeandhealingcenter.org) is an expression of St. Martin's Episcopal Church's vision to minister to those "broken by life's circumstances" and a direct response to the compassionate Great Commission of Jesus. An independent 501c3 nonprofit organization housed on St. Martin's campus, the HHCI is a comprehensive mental health resource serving the Houston community and beyond. Initially operating out of shared office space at the church, the members of St. Martin's conducted a capital campaign and constructed a separate building on campus for the HHCI in 2012.

Staffing: Twenty full-time employees, four part-time employees, and three graduate clinical interns

Partnerships: The HHCI has established partnerships with a wide variety of hospitals, professional organizations, academic institutions, and mental health nonprofit organizations. These include the Houston Methodist Hospital, the Memorial Hermann Hospital, the Menninger Clinic, re:Mind (www.remindsupport.org), the

Alzheimer's Association (www.alz.org), the American Association of Christian Counselors (www.aacc.net), the Council on Recovery (www.councilonrecovery.org), the University of Houston, Houston Baptist University, Baylor University, and the Baylor College of Medicine.

Mission: To build and restore lives to health and wholeness through education, training, clinical services, and research that strengthens the physical, mental, spiritual, and relational health of individuals and families.[4]

Mental Health Services: Clinical and supportive services at the HHCI include telepsychiatry, individual psychotherapy, case management, health-care ethics consultation, grief counseling, a mental health peer-support line, and training and support for caregivers. In addition, the HHCI provides a meeting space for a variety of twelve-step recovery and support groups. All clinical and supportive services are offered free of charge. In addition, the HHCI has developed the Gateway to Hope program (www.mentalhealthgateway.org) to train faith communities to recognize and respond to mental health issues and support the recovery of those living with serious mental illness. Gateway to Hope has gone from being a concept piloted in five low-income zip codes in 2016 to being a network of over a hundred faith communities that span from Port Arthur to Galveston and address mental health-care needs across southeast Texas.

Bethlehem Lutheran Twin Cities (Minneapolis Campus) and St. Joan of Arc Catholic Community

Average Weekend Worship Attendance: 1,000–1,300 (Bethlehem) and 2,300–2,400 (St. Joan of Arc)

Location: Minneapolis, MN (county population 1.3 million)

Setting: Urban

Denomination: Evangelical Lutheran (Bethlehem) and Catholic (St. Joan of Arc)

Website: www.bethlehem-church.org and www.saintjoanofarc.org

History: The mental health collaboration between Bethlehem Lutheran Twin Cities and the St. Joan of Arc Catholic Community began in 2009. A chance meeting of ministry leaders from both churches at a local mental health and faith workshop is where the initial discussions began. Before that year, both churches had successful independent mental health ministries that focused primarily on breaking stigma through education. With the hope of broadening their impact across the city, the churches agreed to form a collaboration, which has now grown to include over twenty faith communities of varying sizes and denominations. While the two churches cohost events, such as a monthly speaker series, they each continue to maintain independent mental health ministries.

Staffing: One full-time employee and thirty-five lay volunteers

Partnerships: The collaboration has formed partnerships with a variety of local mental health organizations, hospitals, and Christian counseling centers, including Vail Place (www.vailplace.org), M Health Fairview Hospital, Mt. Olivet Lutheran Counseling Center, (www.mtolivet.org/counseling), and Westminster Counseling Center (www.westminstercounseling.org).

Mission: The collaboration seeks to help individuals and families gain a greater understanding of mental illness and provide valuable insight into how communities can create supportive environments that foster hope and healing.

Mental Health Services: The collaboration hosts a monthly mental health presentation and a light supper on the second Monday of every month. This event is designed to provide support through resources, education, and social interaction for people living with mental illness, their families and friends, and professionals working in the mental health field. The collaboration has also developed Mental Health Connect (www.mhconnect.org). This service uses trained mental health navigators to assist individuals and families in obtaining mental health treatment, resources, support, and education. In addition, St. Joan of Arc has established a community mental health resource library, and both churches offer support groups.

Eagles View Church

Average Weekend Worship Attendance: 1,000–1,100
Location: Ft. Worth, TX (county population 2.1 million)
Setting: Suburban
Denomination: Nondenominational
Website: www.eaglesviewchurch.org
History: Eagles View Church's HOPE ministry had its beginnings in tragedy.
Following the death of their adult son by suicide in 2013, Bruce and
Debby Barrick began to feel a call to serve those living with mental
illness and their families. In October 2017, they attended the REACH
conference at Saddleback Church. During this three-day event, they
received training on how to start and build a mental health ministry
at their church. After returning from the conference, they shared their
vision for the ministry with the church. Forty church members immediately volunteered to be part of the new ministry. With the full
support of the church's leadership, the HOPE ministry was launched in
the spring of 2018. In support of this new initiative, the senior pastor,
who had personally struggled with depression in the past, began to teach
more on mental health–related topics from the pulpit.
Staffing: Forty to forty-five lay volunteers
Partnerships: The HOPE ministry has developed partnerships with
Saddleback Church and the local chapter of the National Alliance on
Mental Illness (NAMI).
Mission: Extending the radical friendship of Jesus to people and families of
people living with mental unwellness or facing emotional trauma by
providing transforming love, support, and HOPE.
Mental Health Services: The HOPE ministry offers the NAMI Basics
and Family-to-Family educational classes (www.nami.org) for the
caregivers of individuals living with mental illness. In addition, the
ministry offers a wide variety of support groups, including Hope for
Families (for caregivers), Living with Hope (for adults living with
mental illness), Hope Just4Kids (for children in kindergarten through
fifth grade who suffer with mental health problems), Students with

Hope (for middle and high school students feeling hopeless and overwhelmed with life), Veterans with Hope, Conquer Men (for men struggling with sexual integrity), Journey Women (for women who have been hurt by their spouses' struggles with sexual integrity), Conquer for Young Men (for males aged fifteen to nineteen who struggle with sexual integrity), DivorceCare, GriefShare, Embrace Grace (for single mothers with unplanned pregnancies), Living with Chronic Illness, Making Peace with Your Past (for those who want to change patterns of behavior linked to their families of origin), and Survivors of Suicide Loss. The HOPE ministry also refers individuals to local mental health professionals.

Clear Lake Presbyterian Church

Average Weekend Worship Attendance: 400–450
Location: Houston, TX (county population 4.7 million)
Setting: Suburban
Denomination: Presbyterian (USA)
Website: www.clpc.org
History: Clear Lake Presbyterian Church's (CLPC) mental health ministry began in the heart of a single passionate congregant. After returning from a mental health and faith conference, this long-time church member requested a meeting with the clergy and congregational leaders to discuss the importance of CLPC becoming a mental health–equipped church. The leadership was convinced, and the CLPC Mental Wellness Ministry was officially started in 2017. Soon after, sixty-five clergy, congregants, and lay leaders received their initial mental health training through the Hope and Healing Center & Institute's Gateway to Hope program. CLPC then hired a licensed social worker as a part-time mental health journey coordinator to oversee the ministry. Several lay volunteers also received additional training as support-group facilitators and mental health coaches through the Gateway to Hope program. The Mental Wellness

Ministry complements CLPC's long, successful care ministry, which includes Stephen's Ministry, the Gathering Place (a respite for dementia caregivers), and grief support.

Staffing: One part-time employee and ten lay volunteers

Partnerships: The ministry has developed a collaboration with other area churches, and the group meets monthly to discuss mental health issues. In addition, they have formed partnerships with Grace Alliance (www.mentalhealthgracealliance.org), the Hope and Healing Center & Institute, and the Bay Area NET (www.bayareanet.org).

Mission: To integrate mental health awareness and wellness into the life and work of Clear Lake Presbyterian Church.

Mental Health Services: The Mental Wellness Ministry offers support groups for adults and teens struggling with mental health problems as well as twelve-step recovery groups for individuals battling a substance use disorder. One-on-one mental health coaching is also available for those who need individual therapeutic support. Tuesday Topics is an educational seminar presented the first Tuesday of every month that addresses a wide variety of mental health–related issues.

First Church Berkeley

Average Weekend Worship Attendance: 200–225
Location: Berkeley, CA (county population 1.7 million)
Setting: Urban
Denomination: United Church of Christ
Website: www.firstchurchberkeley.org
History: First Church's mental health ministry began as a three-session mental health book study led by the parish nurse in June 2016. The book study was intentionally used to start a conversation on mental health within the congregation. Following the book study, attendees were recruited to help develop a confidentiality statement and a planning guide that was used to frame the mental health ministry. One of the ministry's first actions was to organize mental health "first

aid" training (www.mentalhealthfirstaid.org) at the church for its
volunteers and interested congregants. The mental health ministry
also spearheaded First Church's journey to become a Welcoming,
Inclusive, Supportive, and Engaged (WISE) Congregation for Mental
Health in 2019. The WISE Congregation for Mental Health des-
ignation was adopted by the United Church of Christ in 2015 to
encourage congregations to become more welcoming to individuals
and families living with mental health challenges, brain disorders, and
substance use disorders.

Staffing: Ten lay volunteers

Partnerships: The First Church mental health ministry collaborates with
Pathways to Promise (www.pathways2promise.org) and the UCC
Mental Health Network (www.mhn-ucc.org).

Mission: To encourage their congregation to be welcoming to those living
with mental health challenges, along with their loved ones.

Mental Health Services: The mental health ministry organizes a monthly
educational forum that covers a wide range of mental health–related
topics. The monthly mental health spiritual support group provides
a safe space for those struggling to share their stories in a supportive
faith-based environment. Members of the ministry's companionship
team serve as Sunday morning companions, being present before,
during, and after worship to respond to in-the-moment mental health
challenges such as loneliness, sadness, and confusion.

St. Luke's Episcopal Church

Average Weekend Worship Attendance: 35–45
Location: Livingston, TX (county population 50,031)
Setting: Rural
Denomination: Episcopal
Website: www.stlukeslivingston.org
History: St. Luke's has long served the poor of Polk County through a
resale shop called The Oasis. At one point, the church realized that

many of those accessing this service struggled with mental and behavioral health problems, prompting the vestry to discuss what more the church could do to serve these individuals. These discussions resulted in the formation of the Lake Livingston Area Mental Health Initiative in January 2017. For the first six months, a team of five church members interviewed existing agencies in the community and assessed local mental health needs. This information was used to create a set of short- and long-term goals for the ministry:

Short-Term Goals

- Provide mental and behavioral health training for the public
- Partner with local law enforcement
- Disseminate information on available mental health services within the area

Long-Term Goals

- Develop respite care for caregivers
- Provide transportation for those living with mental and behavioral health problems
- Establish an internship with a local university's graduate social work program

During the second six months of 2017, volunteers in the ministry received training and assistance through the Kaleidoscope Institute (https://www.kscopeinstitute.org/) and the Episcopal Health Foundation (https://www.episcopalhealth.org/), learning how to best implement their proposed ministry plan. To help kick off and promote the mental health ministry, the church's Lenten services focused on mental health.

Staffing: Five lay volunteers

Partnerships: The ministry has developed partnerships with the county probation/parole office, the local housing authority, and Burke Mental Health Services (www.myburke.org).

Mission: To provide hope, support, and care for individuals with mental illness, along with their families and caregivers, in collaboration with community partners. Work to foster a community that will improve overall mental health and break the cycle for the next generation.

Mental Health Services: The mental health ministry offers mental health "first-aid" training (www.mentalhealthfirstaid.org) for adults and teens throughout the year as well as a weekly mental health support group for individuals on probation. In addition, two lay volunteers are being trained as mental health coaches through the American Association of Christian Counselors. Their training will allow them to offer individual therapeutic support. The ministry has also developed a list of local mental health-care providers who have been vetted for referral purposes.

CHARACTERISTICS OF SUCCESSFUL MENTAL HEALTH MINISTRIES

Clearly, mental health ministries can take many forms, depending on the needs and resources of a given faith community. But as these examples demonstrate, it is possible for churches of varying sizes, budgets, locations, and denominations to effectively minister to those living with serious mental illness and their families. In our work with churches across the country, we have found five characteristics common to successful mental health ministries.

Full Support of the Church's Leadership. The church's primary decision-makers, be that a senior pastor, an elder board, or a vestry, see successful mental health ministry as a priority. In these faith communities, leadership not only supports implementing mental health ministry but also fully embraces planning for its growth and development.

Effective Communication. Mental health is a regular part of the congregational conversation. The mental health ministry is regularly presented to the membership in bulletins, emails, and newsletters, and mental health is a common topic of sermons, Sunday school classes, and home groups.

Partnerships. Collaborations and partnerships with mental health nonprofit organizations, academic institutions, and licensed providers outside the church give the mental health ministry opportunities to offer continuing education to its staff and volunteers. Collaborative relationships also provide the ministry with safe, vetted referral sources for those needing professional care.

Passionate Lay Leaders. The ability of a church to recruit, train, and sustain a passionate base of lay volunteers is highly predicative of ministry success. Mental health ministries are often led and staffed by lay volunteers who are zealous about serving those with mental health difficulties as a result of their own lived experiences with mental illness. Churches with successful mental health ministries actively seek these individuals out and empower them for service to others.

A Focus on Community Outreach. Mental health ministries that are developed as an outreach to the local community rather than as a special service available only to church members tend to be more successful. An outreach focus also teaches congregants that mental health is a mission field and provides them with an opportunity to be involved—by bringing in their distressed friends and neighbors for care.

MAKING A DIFFERENCE

God is sending those broken by mental illness to the church. Imagine what could happen if churches were equipped to serve as the front door to the mental health-care system. This would mean that individuals in psychological distress who sought assistance from the church would be quickly identified and referred for professional care.

Now imagine if churches were equipped to be not only effective front doors but also places where therapeutic support was available onsite? These services would not replace professional mental health care but, instead, serve as an adjunct to those resources. Basic interventions, such as psychoeducation, mental health coaching, and support groups, are ideal for implementing in a church setting. Offerings such as these, led by nonprofessionals, have proven to be effective at helping those with mental illness and their families to manage symptoms and maintain stability, and they have the added benefits of minimal cost and maximum accessibility.

Such an imagined scenario is not impossible; the church could potentially transform the mental health-care system. To do so, not every congregation must be involved at the same level, but each congregation must become involved.

Notes

Introduction

1. Jackie L. Goldstein and Marc M. L. Godemont, "The Legend and Lessons of Geel, Belgium: A 1500-Year-Old Legend, a 21st Century Model," *Community Mental Health Journal* 39, no. 5 (2003): 441–458.
2. Substance Abuse and Mental Health Services Administration, *Racial/Ethnic Differences in Mental Health Service Use among Adults*, HHS Publication No. SMA-15-4906 (Rockville, MD: Substance Abuse and Mental Health Services Administration, 2015). Retrieved from https://www.samhsa.gov/data/; Daniel G. Whitney and Mark D. Peterson, "U.S. National and State-Level Prevalence of Mental Health Disorders and Disparities of Mental Health Care Use in Children," *Journal of the American Medical Association: Pediatrics* 172, no. 4 (2019): 389–391.
3. National Alliance for Caregiving, *On Pins and Needles: Caregivers of Adults with Mental Illness* (Washington, DC: National Alliance for Caregiving, 2016). Retrieved from https://www.caregiving.org/; Edward B. Rogers, Matthew S. Stanford, and Diana R. Garland, "The Effects of Mental Illness on Families within Faith Communities," *Mental Health, Religion and Culture* 15, no. 3 (2012): 301–313.
4. Kevin C. Heslin and Audrey J. Weiss, *Hospital Readmissions Involving Psychiatric Disorders, 2012*, HCUP Statistical Brief No. 189 (Rockville, MD: Agency for Healthcare Research and Quality, 2015). Retrieved from https://www.hcup-us.ahrq.gov/reports.jsp.
5. Stefan G. Hofmann et al., "The Efficacy of Cognitive Behavioral Therapy: A Review of Meta-Analyses," *Cognitive Therapy and Research* 36, no. 5 (2012): 427–440; Stefan Leucht et al., "Antipsychotic Drugs versus Placebo for Relapse Prevention in Schizophrenia: A Systematic Review and Meta-Analysis," *The Lancet* 379, no. 9831 (2012): 2063–2071.
6. C. Holly A. Adrilla et al., "Geographic Variation in Supply of Selected Behavioral Health Providers," *American Journal of Preventive Medicine* 54,

no. 6S3 (2018): S199–S207; Health Resources & Services Administration, *Shortage Areas*. Retrieved from https://data.hrsa.gov/topics/health-workforce /shortage-areas.

7. Doris A. Fuller et al., *Going, Going, Gone: Trends and Consequences of Eliminating State Psychiatric Beds, 2016* (Arlington, VA: Treatment Advocacy Center, 2016). Retrieved from https://www.treatmentadvocacycenter.org; World Health Organization, *Mental Health Atlas 2017* (Geneva, Switzerland: World Health Organization, 2018). Retrieved from https://www.who.int /mental_health/evidence/atlas/mental_health_atlas_2017/en/.

8. Kimberly Nordstrom et al., "Boarding of Mentally Ill Patients in Emergency Departments: American Psychiatric Association Resource Document," *Western Journal of Emergency Medicine* 20, no. 5 (2019): 690–695.

9. Cohen Veterans Network and National Council for Behavioral Health, *America's Mental Health 2018*. Retrieved from https://www.cohenveteransnetwork .org/AmericasMentalHealth/.

10. Ibid.

11. Tara F. Bishop et al., "Acceptance of Insurance by Psychiatrists and the Implications for Access to Mental Health Care," *Journal of the American Medical Association: Psychiatry* 71, no. 2 (2014): 176–181.

12. Bernice A. Pescosolido, "The Public Stigma of Mental Illness: What Do We Think; What Do We Know; What Can We Prove?," *Journal of Health and Social Behavior* 54, no. 1 (2013): 1–21.

13. Cohen Veterans Network and National Council for Behavioral Health, *America's Mental Health 2018*. Retrieved from https://www.cohenveteransnetwork .org/AmericasMentalHealth/.

14. Willa D. Meylink and Richard L. Gorsuch, "Relationship between Clergy and Psychologists: The Empirical Data," *Journal of Psychology and Christianity* 7, no. 1 (1988): 56–72; Philip S. Wang, Patricia A. Breglund, and Ronald C. Kessler, "Patterns and Correlates of Contacting Clergy for Mental Disorders in the United States," *Health Services Research* 38, no. 2 (2003): 647–673.

15. H. Paul Chalfant et al., "The Clergy as a Resource for Those Encountering Psychological Distress," *Review of Religious Research* 31, no. 3 (1990): 305–313; Robert J. Taylor et al., "Mental Health Services in Faith Communities: The Role of Clergy in Black Churches," *Social Work* 45, no. 1 (2000): 73–87.

16. Jennifer L. Farrell and Deborah A. Goebert, "Collaboration between Psychiatrists and Clergy in Recognizing and Treating Mental Illness," *Psychiatric Services* 59, no. 4 (2008): 437–440.

17. David B. Larson et al., "The Couch and the Cloth: The Need for Linkage," *Hospital and Community Psychiatry* 39, no. 10 (1988): 1064–1069; Halle E. Ross and Matthew S. Stanford, "Training and Education of North American Master's of Divinity Students in Relation to Serious Mental Illness," *Journal of Research on Christian Education* 23, no. 2 (2014): 176–186.

18. Meylink and Gorsuch, "Relationship between Clergy and Psychologists," 57.

19. LifeWay Research, *Study of Acute Mental Illness and Christian Faith: Research Report* (2014). Retrieved from http://lifewayresearch.com/mentalillnessstudy/.

20. Psychological distress is a general term used to describe a set of unpleasant thoughts, feelings, and/or emotions that negatively impact an individual's level of functioning.

Chapter 1

1. Tom Cruise, interview by Larry King, *Larry King Live*, CNN, November 28, 2003, transcript retrieved from http://transcripts.cnn.com/TRANSCRIPTS/0311/28/lkl.00.html; Tom Cruise, interview by Matt Lauer, *Today Show*, NBC, June 24, 2005, transcript retrieved from https://www.today.com/popculture/im-passionate-about-life-wbna8343367.

2. Matthew S. Stanford, *Grace for the Afflicted: A Clinical and Biblical Perspective on Mental Illness, Revised & Expanded* (Downers Grove, IL: InterVarsity, 2017).

3. World Health Organization, *Mental Health: Strengthening Mental Health Promotion* (Geneva, Switzerland: World Health Organization, 2018). Retrieved from https://www.who.int/news-room/fact-sheets/detail/mental-health-strengthening-our-response.

4. Stanford, *Grace for the Afflicted*.

5. American Psychiatric Association, *Diagnostic and Statistical Manual of Mental Disorders, Fifth Edition* (Washington, DC: American Psychiatric Association, 2013) (hereafter cited as APA, *DSM-5*).

6. Robert M. McCarron, "The DSM-5 and the Art of Medicine: Certainly Uncertain," *Annals of Internal Medicine* 159, no. 5 (2013): 360–361.

7. Ronald Pies, "How 'Objective' Are Psychiatric Diagnoses? (Guess Again)," *Psychiatry* 4, no. 10 (2007): 18–22.

8. Ronald C. Kessler et al., "Lifetime Prevalence and Age-of-Onset Distributions of Mental Disorders in the World Health Organization's World Mental Health Survey Initiative," *World Psychiatry* 6, no. 3 (2007): 168–176.

9. Ronald C. Kessler et al., "Prevalence, Severity, and Comorbidity of 12-Month DSM-IV Disorders in the National Comorbidity Survey Replication," *Archives of General Psychiatry* 62, no. 6 (2005): 617–627.

10. APA, *DSM-5*.

11. National Alliance on Mental Illness, "Mental Health by the Numbers," 2019. Retrieved from https://www.nami.org/learn-more/mental-health-by-the -numbers.

12. APA, *DSM-5*.

13. Substance Abuse and Mental Health Services Administration, *Key Substance Use and Mental Health Indicators in the United States: Results from the 2018 National Survey on Drug Use and Health,* HHS Publication No. PEP19-5068, NSDUH Series H-54 (Rockville, MD: Substance Abuse and Mental Health Services Administration, 2019). Retrieved from https://www.samhsa.gov/data/.

14. APA, *DSM-5*.

15. Ibid.

16. Andreas Maercker et al., "Adjustment Disorders: Prevalence in a Representative Nationwide Survey in Germany," *Social Psychiatry and Psychiatric Epidemiology* 47, no. 11 (2012): 1745–1752; Risë B. Goldstein et al., "The Epidemiology of DSM-5 Posttraumatic Stress Disorder in the United States: Results from the National Epidemiologic Survey on Alcohol and Related Conditions III," *Social Psychiatry and Psychiatric Epidemiology* 51, no. 8 (2016): 1137–1148.

17. Tomoko Udo and Carlos M. Grilo, "Prevalence and Correlates of DSM-5— Defined Eating Disorders in a Nationally Representative Sample of U.S. Adults," *Biological Psychiatry* 84, no. 5 (2018): 345–354.

18. APA, *DSM-5*.

19. Ibid.

20. Jason C. Simeone et al., "An Evaluation of Variation in Published Estimates of Schizophrenia Prevalence from 1990–2013: A Systematic Literature Review," *BMC Psychiatry* 15 (2015): 193; Berta Moreno-Kuestner et al., "Prevalence of Psychotic Disorders and Its Association with Methodological Issues: A Systematic Review and Meta-Analyses," *PLoS ONE* 13, no. 4 (2018): e0195687.

21. Pamela L. Owens et al., *Inpatient Stays Involving Mental and Substance Use Disorders, 2016,* HCUP Statistical Brief No. 249 (Rockville, MD: Agency for Healthcare Research and Quality, 2019). Retrieved from https://www.hcup-us .ahrq.gov/.

22. Michael Hendryx et al., "Social Support, Activities, and Recovery from Serious Mental Illness: STARS Study Findings," *Journal of Behavioral Health Services & Research* 36, no. 3 (2009): 320–329.

23. Courtenay M. Harding et al., "The Vermont Longitudinal Study of Persons with Severe Mental Illness I: Methodology, Study Sample, and Overall Status 32 Years Later," *American Journal of Psychiatry* 144, no. 6 (1987): 718–726; Mark S. Salzer et al., "National Estimates of Recovery-Remission from Serious Mental Illness," *Psychiatric Services* 69, no. 5 (2018): 523–528.

Chapter 2

1. Jennifer L. Farrell and Deborah A. Goebert, "Collaboration between Psychiatrists and Clergy in Recognizing and Treating Mental Illness," *Psychiatric Services* 59, no. 4 (2008): 437–440.
2. Philip S. Wang, Patricia A. Breglund, and Ronald C. Kessler, "Patterns and Correlates of Contacting Clergy for Mental Disorders in the United States," *Health Services Research* 38, no. 2 (2003): 647–673.
3. LifeWay Research, *Pastors' Views on Opioid Abuse: Survey of American Protestant Pastors* (2018). Retrieved from http://lifewayresearch.com/wp -content/uploads/2019/11/Report-Pastors-Sept-2018-Opioid-Abuse.pdf.
4. Substance Abuse and Mental Health Services Administration, *Key Substance Use and Mental Health Indicators in the United States: Results from the 2018 National Survey on Drug Use and Health*, HHS Publication No. PEP19-5068, NSDUH Series H-54 (Rockville, MD: Substance Abuse and Mental Health Services Administration, 2019). Retrieved from https://www.samhsa.gov/data/.
5. John A. Ewing, "Detecting Alcoholism: The CAGE Questionnaire," *Journal of the American Medical Association* 252, no. 14 (1984): 1905–1907; Richard L. Brown and Laura A. Rounds, "Conjoint Screening Questionnaires for Alcohol and Other Drug Abuse: Criterion Validity in a Primary Care Practice," *Wisconsin Medical Journal* 94, no. 3 (1995): 135–140.
6. Ronald C. Kessler et al., "Short Screening Scales to Monitor Population Prevalences and Trends in Non-Specific Psychological Distress," *Psychological Medicine* 32, no. 6 (2002): 959–976.

Chapter 3

1. Centers for Disease Control and Prevention, "Mental-Health Surveillance among Children—United States, 2005–2011," *Morbidity and Mortality Weekly Report* 62, no. 2 (2013): 1–35; Ronald C. Kessler et al., "Age of Onset

of Mental Disorders: A Review of Recent Literature," *Current Opinion in Psychiatry* 20, no. 4 (2007): 359–364.

2. Philip S. Wang et al., "Delays in Initial Treatment Contact after First Onset of a Mental Disorder," *Health Services Research* 39, no. 2 (2004): 393–416.

3. Daniel G. Whitney and Mark D. Peterson, "U.S. National and State-Level Prevalence of Mental Health Disorders and Disparities of Mental Health-Care Use in Children," *JAMA Pediatrics* 173, no. 4 (2019): 389–391.

4. Melonie Heron, "Deaths: Leading Causes for 2017," *National Vital Statistics Reports* 68, no. 6 (2019): 1–77.

5. Kathleen R. Merikangas et al., "Lifetime Prevalence of Mental Disorders in U.S. Adolescents: Results from the National Comorbidity Survey Replication—Adolescent Supplement (NCS-A)," *Journal of American Academy of Child and Adolescent Psychiatry* 49, no. 10 (2010): 980–989.

6. Melissa L. Danielson et al., "Prevalence of Parent-Reported ADHD Diagnosis and Associated Treatment among U.S. Children and Adolescents, 2016," *Journal of Clinical Child and Adolescent Psychology* 47, no. 2 (2018): 199–212; APA, *DSM-5.*

7. Reem M. Ghandour et al., "Prevalence and Treatment of Depression, Anxiety, and Conduct Problems in U.S. Children," *Journal of Pediatrics* 206, e3 (2019): 256–267; APA, *DSM-5.*

8. Merikangas et al., "Lifetime Prevalence of Mental Disorders in U.S. Adolescents," 980–989; APA, *DSM-5*; Sung E. Son and Jeffrey T. Kirchner, "Depression in Children and Adolescents," *American Family Physician* 62, no. 10 (2000): 2297–2308.

9. APA, *DSM-5*; Ruth Perou et al., "Mental Health Surveillance among Children—United States, 2005–2011," *MMWR Morbidity and Mortality Weekly Report* 62, no. 2 (2013): 1–35.

10. Matthew J. Maenner et al., "Prevalence of Autism Spectrum Disorder among Children Aged 8 Years—Autism and Developmental Disabilities Monitoring Network, 11 Sites, United States, 2016," *MMWR Surveillance Summaries* 69, no. 4 (2020): 1–12; Michael D. Kogan et al., "The Prevalence of Parent-Reported Autism Spectrum Disorder among U.S. Children," *Pediatrics* 142, no. 6 (2018): e20174161; APA, *DSM-5.*

11. Gordon Parker et al., "The Development of a Brief Screening Measure of Emotional Distress in Children," *Journal of Child Psychology and Psychiatry* 42, no. 2 (2001): 221–225.

12. Shannon L. Stewart and Chloe A. Hamza, "The Child and Youth Mental Health Assessment (ChYMH): An Examination of the Psychometric

Properties of an Integrated Assessment Developed for Clinically Referred Children and Youth," *BMC Health Services Research* 17, no. 1 (2017): 82.

13. Stewart and Hamza, "The Child and Youth Mental Health Assessment (ChYMH)," 82.

14. Peter M. Lewinsohn et al., "The OADP-CDS: A Brief Screener for Adolescent Conduct Disorder," *Journal of the American Academy of Child and Adolescent Psychiatry* 39, no. 7 (2000): 888–895.

Chapter 4

1. LifeWay Research, *Suicide and the Church* (2017). Retrieved from http://lifewayresearch.com/wp-content/uploads/2017/09/Suicide-and-the-Church-Research-Study-Report.pdf.

2. Jamie Ducharme, "U.S. Suicide Rates Are the Highest They've Been Since World War II," *Time*, June 10, 2019. Retrieved from https://time.com/5609124/us-suicide-rate-increase/.

3. National Institute of Mental Health, "Suicide." Retrieved January 29, 2020, from https://www.nimh.nih.gov/health/statistics/suicide.shtml.

4. Substance Abuse and Mental Health Services Administration, *Key Substance Use and Mental Health Indicators in the United States: Results from the 2018 National Survey on Drug Use and Health*, HHS Publication No. PEP19-5068, NSDUH Series H-54 (Rockville, MD: Substance Abuse and Mental Health Services Administration, 2019). Retrieved from https://www.samhsa.gov/data/.

5. Ibid.

6. American Foundation for Suicide Prevention, "Suicide Statistics." Retrieved January 29, 2020, from https://afsp.org/about-suicide/suicide-statistics/.

7. Geneviève Arsenault-Lapierre et al., "Psychiatric Diagnoses in 3275 Suicides: A Meta-Analysis," *BMC Psychiatry* 4, no. 37 (2004). Retrieved from https://doi.org/10.1186/1471-244X-4-37; Jonathan T. O. Cavanagh et al., "Psychological Autopsy Studies of Suicide: A Systematic Review," *Psychological Medicine* 33, no. 3 (2003): 395–405.

8. Edward Chesney et al., "Risks of All-Cause and Suicide Mortality in Mental Disorders: A Meta-Review," *World Psychiatry* 13, no. 4 (2014): 153–160.

9. Matthew K. Nock et al., "Cross-National Prevalence and Risk Factors for Suicidal Ideation, Plans, and Attempts," *British Journal of Psychiatry* 192, no. 2 (2008): 98–105.

10. Robert C. Kessler et al., "Prevalence of and Risk Factors for Lifetime Suicide Attempts in the National Comorbidity Survey," *Archives of General Psychiatry* 56, no. 7 (1999): 617–626.

11. Caroline A. Blades et al., "The Benefits and Risks of Asking Research Participants about Suicide: A Meta-Analysis of the Impact of Exposure to Suicide-Related Content," *Clinical Psychology Review* 64, August (2018): 1–12; T. Dazzi et al., "Does Asking about Suicide and Related Behaviors Induce Suicidal Ideation? What Is the Evidence?," *Psychological Medicine* 44, no. 16 (2014): 3361–3363.

12. Keith Hawtdn et al., "Suicide in Young People: Study of 174 Cases, Aged under 25 years, Based on Coroners and Medical Records," *British Journal of Psychiatry* 175, no. 3 (1999): 271–276; Kjell E. Rudestam, "Stockholm and Los Angeles: A Cross-Cultural Study of the Communication of Suicidal Intent," *Journal of Consulting and Clinical Psychology* 36, no. 1 (1971): 82–90.

13. Daniel T. Chung et al., "Suicide Rates after Discharge from Psychiatric Facilities: A Systematic Review and Meta-Analysis," *JAMA Psychiatry* 74, no. 7 (2017): 694–702; Michael Goldacre et al., "Suicide after Discharge from Psychiatric Inpatient Care," *The Lancet* 342, no. 8866 (1993): 283–286.

14. Robert I. Simon, "Imminent Suicide: The Illusion of Short-Term Prediction," *Suicide and Life-Threatening Behavior* 36, no. 3 (2006): 296–301.

Chapter 5

1. Bernice A. Pescosolido et al., "Evolving Public Views on the Likelihood of Violence from People with Mental Illness: Stigma and Its Consequences," *Health Affairs* 38, no. 10 (2019): 1735–1743.

2. CNN, "Trump Remarks on Deadly Texas Shooting," November 6, 2017. Retrieved from https://www.cnn.com/videos/politics/2017/11/06/president -trump-sutherland-texas-church-shooting-full-remarks.cnn.

3. Heather Stuart and Julio Arboleda-Flórez, "A Public Health Perspective on Violent Offenses among Persons with Mental Illness," *Psychiatric Services* 52, no. 5 (2001): 654–659; Jeffrey W. Swanson, "Mental Disorder, Substance Abuse, and Community Violence: An Epidemiological Approach," in *Violence and Mental Disorder: Developments in Risk Assessment*, ed., John Monahan and Henry J. Steadman (Chicago, IL: University of Chicago Press, 1994).

4. Marvin S. Swartz and Sayanti Bhattacharya, "Victimization of Persons with Severe Mental Illness: A Pressing Global Health Problem," *World Psychiatry* 16,

no. 1 (2017): 26–27; Virginia A. Hiday et al., "Criminal Victimization of Persons with Severe Mental Illness," *Psychiatric Services* 50, no. 1 (1999): 62–88.

5. John Monahan et al., *Rethinking Risk Assessment: The MacArthur Study of Mental Disorder and Violence* (New York: Oxford University Press, 2001); Henry J. Steadman et al., "Violence by People Discharged from Acute Psychiatric Inpatient Facilities and by Others in the Same Neighborhoods," *Archives of General Psychiatry* 55, no. 5 (1998): 393–401.

6. Katrina Witt et al., "Risk Factors for Violence in Psychosis: Systematic Review and Meta-Regression Analysis of 110 Studies," *PLoS ONE* 8, no. 2 (2013): e55942; John Monahan et al., *Rethinking Risk Assessment: The MacArthur Study of Mental Disorder and Violence* (New York: Oxford University Press, 2001); Jeffrey W. Swanson et al., "Violence and Psychiatric Disorder in the Community: Evidence from the Epidemiologic Catchment Area Surveys," *Hospital and Community Psychiatry* 41, no. 7 (1990): 761–770.

7. William J. Krouse and Daniel J. Richardson, "Mass Murder with Firearms: Incidents and Victims, 1999–2013," *Congressional Research Service Report* R44126, July 30, 2015. Retrieved from https://fas.org/sgp/crs/misc/R44126 .pdf.

8. National Council for Behavioral Health, "Mass Violence in America: Causes, Impacts, and Solutions," August 2019. Retrieved from https://www .thenationalcouncil.org/wp-content/uploads/2019/08/Mass-Violence-in -America_8-6-19.pdf?daf=375ateTbd56.

9. The Violence Project, *Mass Shooting Database*. Available at https://www .theviolenceproject.org/.

10. Rebecca J. Houston et al., "Neurobiological Correlates and Clinical Implications of Aggressive Subtypes," *Journal of Forensic Neuropsychology* 3, no. 4 (2003): 67–87.

11. Matthew S. Stanford et al., "Characterizing Aggressive Behavior," *Assessment* 10, no. 2 (2003): 183–190.

12. APA, *DSM-5*.

13. Andrew Harris and Arthur J. Lurigio, "Mental Illness and Violence: A Brief Review of Research and Assessment Strategies," *Aggression and Violent Behavior* 12, no. 5 (2007): 542–551.

14. Rongqin Yu et al., "Personality Disorders, Violence, and Antisocial Behavior: A Systematic Review and Meta-Regression Analysis," *Journal of Personality Disorders* 26, no. 5 (2012): 775–792.

15. Lawrence A. Greenfeld and Tracy L. Snell, *Women Offenders*, Bureau of Justice Statistics Special Report No. NCJ 175688 (Washington, DC: U.S. Department of Justice, 1999).

16. W. Huw Williams et al., "Traumatic Brain Injury: A Potential Cause of Violent Crime?," *Lancet Psychiatry* 5, no. 10 (2018): 836–844.

17. Raymond W. Novaco, "Anger Dysregulation: Driver of Violent Offending," *Journal of Forensic Psychiatry & Psychology* 22, no. 5 (2011): 650–668.

18. Dale E. McNiel et al., "The Relationship between Command Hallucinations and Violence," *Psychiatric Services* 51, no. 10 (2000): 1288–1292.

19. Henry J. Steadman and Stephen A. Ribner, "Life Stress and Violence among Ex-Mental Patients," *Social Science & Medicine* 16, no. 18 (1982): 1641–1647.

20. Hanna Sahlin et al., "Association between Deliberate Self-Harm and Violent Criminality," *JAMA Psychiatry* 74, no. 6 (2017): 615–621; Katrina Witt et al., "The Relationship between Suicide and Violence in Schizophrenia: Analysis of the Clinical Antipsychotic Trials of Intervention Effectiveness (CATIE) Dataset," *Schizophrenia Research* 154, no. 1–3 (2014): 61–67.

21. Ernest S. Barratt et al., "Impulsive and Premeditated Aggression: A Factor Analysis of Self-Reported Acts," *Psychiatry Research* 86, no. 2 (1999): 163–173.

Chapter 6

1. Willa D. Meylink and Richard L. Gorsuch, "Relationship between Clergy and Psychologists: The Empirical Data," *Journal of Psychology and Christianity* 7, no. 1 (1988): 56–72.

2. David B. Larson et al., "The Couch and the Cloth: The Need for Linkage," *Hospital and Community Psychiatry* 39, no. 10 (1988): 1064–1069.

3. Mark R. McMinn and Amy W. Dominguez, eds., *Psychology and the Church* (Hauppauge, NY: Nova Science Publishers, 2005).

4. Matthew S. Stanford and David Philpott, "Baptist Senior Pastors' Knowledge and Perceptions of Mental Illness," *Mental Health, Religion & Culture* 14, no. 3 (2011): 281–290; Mark R. McMinn et al., "Factors Affecting Clergy-Psychologist Referral Patterns," *Journal of Psychology and Theology* 33, no. 4 (2005): 299–309.

5. Graham Thornicroft, "Stigma and Discrimination Limit Access to Mental Health Care," *Epidemiology and Psychiatric Sciences* 17, no. 1 (2008): 14–19.

6. A court order is not required to determine that a person lacks mental capacity. Discretion lies with the mental health-care provider, based on professional judgment.
7. Edward B. Rogers and Matthew S. Stanford, "A Church-Based Peer-Led Group Intervention for Mental Illness," *Mental Health, Religion & Culture* 18, no. 6 (2015): 470–481; Paul N. Pfeiffer et al., "Efficacy of Peer Support Interventions for Depression: A Meta-Analysis," *General Hospital Psychiatry* 33, no. 1 (2011): 29–36.

Chapter 7

1. Tuan M. Tran et al., "Psychosis with Paranoid Delusions after a Therapeutic Dose of Mefloquine: A Case Report," *Malaria Journal* 5, article no. 74 (2006).
2. Christopher C. H. Cook, "Religious Psychopathology: The Prevalence of Religious Content of Delusions and Hallucinations in Mental Disorder," *International Journal of Social Psychiatry* 61, no. 4 (2015): 404–425; Harold G. Koenig, "Religion, Spirituality and Psychotic Disorders," *Archives of Clinical Psychiatry* 34, no. 1 (2007): 40–48; Ronald Siddle et al., "Religious Delusions in Patients Admitted to Hospital with Schizophrenia," *Social Psychiatry and Psychiatric Epidemiology* 37, no. 3 (2002): 130–138.
3. Eva Ouwehand et al., "Holy Apparition or Hyper-Religiosity: Prevalence of Explanatory Models for Religious and Spiritual Experiences in Patients with Bipolar Disorder and Their Associations with Religiousness," *Pastoral Psychology* 69, no. 1 (2020): 29–45; Johnathan S. Abramowitz and Ryan J. Jacoby, "Scrupulosity: A Cognitive-Behavioral Analysis and Implications for Treatment," *Journal of Obsessive-Compulsive and Related Disorders* 3, no. 2 (2014): 14–149; Eva Ouwehand et al., "The Awful Rowing toward God: Interpretation of Religious Experiences by Individuals with Bipolar Disorder," *Pastoral Psychology* 68, no. 4 (2019): 437–462.
4. Raphael M. Bonelli and Harold G. Koenig, "Mental Disorders, Religion and Spirituality, 1990 to 2010: A Systematic Evidence-Based Review," *Journal of Religion and Health* 52, no. 2 (2013): 657–673.
5. George Kirov et al., "Religious Faith after Psychotic Illness," *Psychopathology* 31, no. 5 (1998): 234–245; George Fitchett et al., "The Religious Needs and Resources of Psychiatric Inpatients," *Journal of Nervous and Mental Disease* 185, no. 5 (1997): 320–326.

6. David Lukoff, "Spirituality in Recovery from Persistent Mental Disorders," *Southern Medical Journal* 100, no. 6 (2007): 642–646.

7. Edward B. Rogers and Matthew S. Stanford, "A Church-Based Peer-Led Group Intervention for Mental Illness," *Mental Health, Religion & Culture* 18, no. 6 (2015): 470–481.

Chapter 8

1. World Health Organization, *World Health Report 2001: Mental Health: New Understanding, New Hope* (Geneva, Switzerland: WHO, 2001). Retrieved from https://www.who.int/whr/2001/en/.

2. National Alliance for Caregiving, *On Pins & Needles: Caregivers of Adults with Mental Illness* (Washington, DC: National Alliance for Caregiving, 2016). Retrieved from https://www.caregiving.org/.

3. Gayle D. Gubman and Richard C. Tessler, "The Impact of Mental Illness on Families: Concepts and Priorities," *Journal of Family Issues* 8, no. 2 (1987): 226–245.

4. Edie Mannion, "Resilience and Burden in Spouses of People with Mental Illness," *Psychiatric Rehabilitation Journal* 20, no. 2 (1996): 13–23.

5. National Alliance for Caregiving, *On Pins & Needles*.

6. Gubman and Tessler, "The Impact of Mental Illness on Families," 229.

7. Mariann Idstad et al., "Mental Disorder and Caregiver Burden in Spouses: The Nord-Trøndelag Health Study," *BMC Public Health* 10, no. 516 (2010). Retrieved from https://doi.org/10.1186/1471-2458-10–516; Mannion, "Resilience and Burden in Spouses of People with Mental Illness," 15.

8. Edward B. Rogers et al., "The Effects of Mental Illness on Families within Faith Communities," *Mental Health, Religion & Culture* 15, no. 3 (2012): 301–313.

9. Wubalem Fekadu et al., "Multidimensional Impact of Severe Mental Illness on Family Members: Systematic Review," *BMJ Open* 9, e032391 (2019). Retrieved from https://doi.org/10.1136/bmjopen-2019-032391; Jana C. Saunders, "Families Living with Severe Mental Illness: A Literature Review," *Issues in Mental Health Nursing* 24, no. 2 (2003): 175–198.

10. National Alliance for Caregiving, *On Pins & Needles*.

11. Saunders, "Families Living with Severe Mental Illness: A Literature Review," 175–198.

12. Robert Bland and Yvonne Darlington, "The Nature and Sources of Hope: Perspectives of Family Caregivers of People with Serious Mental Illness," *Perspectives in Psychiatric Care* 38, no. 2 (2009): 61–68; Eric D. Johnson, "Differences among Families Coping with Serious Mental Illness: A Qualitative Analysis," *American Journal of Orthopsychiatry* 70, no. 1 (2000): 126–134.

13. Aaron B. Murray-Swank et al., "Religiosity, Psychosocial Adjustment, and Subjective Burden of Persons Who Care for Those with Mental Illness," *Psychiatric Services* 57, no. 3 (2006): 361–365.

14. Kenneth I. Pargament, "Religious Methods of Coping: Resources for the Conservation and Transformation of Significance," in *Religion and the Clinical Practice of Psychology*, ed., Edward P. Shafranske (Washington, DC: American Psychological Association, 1996).

15. Paul K. Maciejewski et al., "An Empirical Examination of the Stage Theory of Grief," *Journal of the American Medical Association* 297, no. 7 (2007): 716–723; Elizabeth Kubler-Ross and David Kessler, *On Grief and Grieving: Finding the Meaning of Grief through the Five Stages of Loss* (New York: Scribner, 2005).

16. P. Jane Milliken, "Disenfranchised Mothers: Caring for an Adult Child with Schizophrenia," *Health Care for Women International* 22, no. 1–2 (2001): 149–166; Anita Pejlert, "Being a Parent of an Adult Son or Daughter with Severe Mental Illness Receiving Professional Care: Parents' Narratives," *Health and Social Care in the Community* 9, no. 4 (2001): 194–204; Harriet P. Lefley, "Aging Parents as Caregivers of Mentally Ill Adult Children: An Emerging Social Problem," *Hospital and Community Psychiatry* 38, no. 10 (1987): 1063–1070.

17. Mary M. Doornbos, "The Problems and Coping Methods of Caregivers of Young Adults with Mental Illness," *Journal of Psychosocial Nursing and Mental Health Services* 35, no. 9 (1997): 22–26; Jane S. Norbeck et al., "Social Support Needs of Family Caregivers of Psychiatric Patients from Three Age Groups," *Nursing Research* 40, no. 4 (1991): 208–213; Lefley, "Aging Parents as Caregivers of Mentally Ill Adult Children: An Emerging Social Problem," 1063–1070.

18. Rogers et al., "The Effects of Mental Illness on Families within Faith Communities," 301–313.

19. Farkhondeh Sharif et al., "Effect of a Psycho-Educational Intervention for Family Members on Caregiver Burdens and Psychiatric Symptoms in Patients with Schizophrenia in Shiraz, Iran," *BMC Psychiatry* 12, no. 48 (2012). Retrieved

from https://doi.org/10.1186/1471-244X-12-48; William R. McFarlane et al.,
"Family Psychoeducation and Schizophrenia: A Review of the Literature,"
Journal of Marital and Family Therapy 29, no. 2 (2003): 223–245.

Chapter 9

1. LifeWay Research, *Study of Acute Mental Illness and Christian Faith: Research Report* (2014). Retrieved from http://lifewayresearch.com/mentalillnessstudy/.
2. Amy Simpson, *Troubled Minds: Mental Illness and the Church's Mission* (Downers Grove, IL: Intervarsity, 2013).
3. Diana Rose et al., "250 Labels Used to Stigmatize People with Mental Illness," *BMC Health Services Research* 7, no. 97 (2007). Retrieved from https://doi.org /10.1186/1472-6963-7-97.
4. Patricia B. Nemec et al., "Can You Hear Me Now? Teaching Listening Skills," *Psychiatric Rehabilitation Journal* 40, no. 4 (2017): 415–417; Kathryn Robertson, "Active Listening: More Than Just Paying Attention," *Australian Family Physician* 34, no. 12 (2005): 1053–1055.
5. Janet S. Richmond et al., "Verbal De-Escalation of the Agitated Patient: Consensus Statement of the American Association for Emergency Psychiatry Project BETA De-Escalation Workgroup," *Western Journal of Emergency Medicine* 8, no. 1 (2012): 17–25.

Chapter 10

1. Matthew S. Stanford et al., "Feasibility and Efficacy of a Peer-Led Group Recovery Program for War-Related Trauma in Libya," *South African Journal of Psychology* 44, no. 1 (2014): 97–105.
2. Phuong Thao D. Le et al., "Health Issues Associated with Commercial Sexual Exploitation and Sex Trafficking of Children in the United States: A Systematic Review," *Behavioral Medicine* 44, no. 3 (2018): 219–233; Seth J. Prins, "The Prevalence of Mental Illnesses in U.S. State Prisons: A Systematic Review," *Psychiatric Services* 65, no. 7 (2014): 862–872; Maryann Davis et al., "Prevalence and Impact of Substance Use among Emerging Adults with Serious Mental Health Conditions," *Psychiatric Rehabilitation Journal* 35, no. 3 (2012): 235–243; Carol S. North et al., "Are Rates of Psychiatric Disorders in

the Homeless Population Changing?," *American Journal of Public Health* 94, no. 1 (2004): 103–108.

3. Substance Abuse and Mental Health Services Administration, *Key Substance Use and Mental Health Indicators in the United States: Results from the 2018 National Survey on Drug Use and Health*, HHS Publication No. PEP19-5068, NSDUH Series H-54 (Rockville, MD: Substance Abuse and Mental Health Services Administration, 2019). Retrieved from https://www.samhsa.gov/data/; APA, *DSM-5*.

4. Blessed Ajegena et al., "Sex and Sexual Addiction in the United States of America: An Overview of its Epidemiology, Management and Prevention Strategies," *Journal of Addiction Research & Therapy* 9, no. 5 (2018): 366. Retrieved from https://doi.org/10.4172/2155-6105.1000366; Richard B. Krueger and Meg S. Kaplan, "The Paraphilic and Hypersexual Disorders: An Overview," *Journal of Psychiatric Practice* 7, no. 6 (2001): 391–403.

5. Claudio Imperatori et al., "Food Addiction: Definition, Measurement and Prevalence in Healthy Subjects and in Patients with Eating Disorders," *Rivista di Psichiatria* 51, no. 2 (2016): 60–65; Barna Konkolÿ Thege et al., "Natural Course of Behavioral Addictions: A 5-year Longitudinal Study," *BMC Psychiatry* 22, no. 15 (2015): 4. Retrieved from https://doi.org/10.1186/s12888-015-0383-3; APA, *DSM-5*.

6. Yvonne H. C. Yau and Marc N. Potenza, "Gambling Disorder and Other Behavioral Addictions: Recognition and Treatment," *Harvard Review of Psychiatry* 23, no. 2 (2015): 134–146; APA, *DSM-5*.

7. David C. Hodgins and Nady el-Guebaly, "Retrospective and Prospective Reports of Precipitants to Relapse in Pathological Gambling," *Journal of Consulting and Clinical Psychology* 72, no. 1 (2004): 72–80; A. Thomas McLellan et al., "Drug Dependence, a Chronic Medical Illness: Implications for Treatment, Insurance, and Outcomes Evaluation," *Journal of the American Medical Association* 284, no. 13 (2000): 1689–1695; Jennifer P. Schneider et al., "Disclosure of Extramarital Sexual Activities by Sexually Exploitative Professionals and Other Persons with Addictive and Compulsive Sexual Disorders," *Journal of Sex Education and Therapy* 24, no. 4 (2000): 277–287; W. Stewart Agras et al., "One-Year Follow-Up of Cognitive-Behavioral Therapy for Obese Individuals with Binge Eating Disorder," *Journal of Consulting and Clinical Psychology* 65, no. 2 (1997): 343–347.

8. Susan R. Tate et al., "Context of Relapse for Substance-Dependent Adults with and without Comorbid Psychiatric Disorders," *Addictive Behaviors* 29, no. 9

(2004): 1707–1724; Kristin L. Tomlinson et al., "Psychiatric Comorbidity and Substance Use Treatment Outcomes of Adolescents," *Psychology of Addictive Behaviors* 18, no. 2 (2004): 160–169.

9. Danielle Kaeble and Mary Cowhig, *Correctional Populations in the United States, 2016*, Bureau of Justice Statistics Publication No. NCJ 251211 (Washington, DC: U.S. Department of Justice, 2018).

10. Treatment Advocacy Center, "Serious Mental Illness (SMI) Prevalence in Jails and Prisons," September 2016. Retrieved from https://www.treatmentadvocacycenter.org/evidence-and-research/learn-more-about/3695; Doris J. James and Lauren E. Glaze, *Mental Health Problems of Prison and Jail Inmates*, Bureau of Justice Statistics Publication No. NCJ 213600 (Washington, DC: U.S. Department of Justice, 2006).

11. APA, *DSM-5*.

12. Diane Langberg, "How to Develop an Effective Trauma Recovery Ministry," in *The Struggle Is Real: How to Care for Mental and Relational Needs in the Church*, ed., Tim Clinton and Jared Pingleton (Bloomington, IN: WestBow, 2017), 224.

13. Evelyn J. Bromet et al., "Post-Traumatic Stress Disorder Associated with Natural and Human-Made Disasters in the World Mental Health Surveys," *Psychological Medicine* 47, no. 2 (2017): 227–241; Carol S. North, "Current Research and Recent Breakthroughs on the Mental Health Effects of Disasters," *Current Psychiatry Reports* 16, no. 481 (2014). Retrieved from https://doi.org/10.1007/s11920-014-0481-9; Yuval Neria et al., "Post-Traumatic Stress Disorder Following Disasters: A Systematic Review," *Psychological Medicine* 38, no. 4 (2008): 467–480.

14. Victims of Trafficking and Violence Protection Act of 2000, Pub. L. No. 106–386, H.R. 3244 (October 28, 2000). Retrieved from https://2009-2017.state.gov/j/tip/laws/61124.htm.

15. National Human Trafficking Hotline, "Hotline Statistics." Retrieved from https://humantraffickinghotline.org/states; U.S. Department of State, *2002 Trafficking in Persons Report*, June 5, 2002. Retrieved from https://2009-2017.state.gov/documents/organization/10815.pdf.

16. Elizabeth K. Hopper and Lucia D. Gonzalez, "A Comparison of Psychological Symptoms in Survivors of Sex and Labor Trafficking," *Behavioral Medicine* 44, no. 3 (2018): 177–188; Cathy Zimmerman et al., "The Health of Trafficked Women: A Survey of Women Entering Posttrafficking Services in Europe," *American Journal of Public Health* 98, no. 1 (2008): 55–59.

17. Centers for Disease Control and Prevention, *The National Intimate Partner and Sexual Violence Survey (NISVS): 2010–2012 State Report* (Atlanta, GA: National Center for Injury Prevention and Control, CDC, 2017).

18. Jacquelyn C. Campbell, "Health Consequences of Intimate Partner Violence," *Lancet* 359, no. 9314 (2002): 1331–1336; Jacqueline M. Golding, "Intimate Partner Violence as a Risk Factor for Mental Disorders: A Meta-Analysis," *Journal of Family Violence* 14, no. 2 (1999): 99–132.

19. APA, *DSM-5*; Terri Tanielian and Lisa H. Jaycox, *Invisible Wounds of War: Psychological and Cognitive Injuries, Their Consequences, and Services to Assist Recovery* (Santa Monica, CA: RAND Corporation, 2008); Han K. Kang et al., "Post-Traumatic Stress Disorder and Chronic Fatigue Syndrome-Like Illness among Gulf War Veterans: A Population-Based Survey of 30,000 Veterans," *American Journal of Epidemiology* 157, no. 2 (2003): 141–148; Richard A. Kulka et al., *The National Vietnam Veterans Readjustment Study: Tables of Findings and Technical Appendices* (New York: Brunner/Mazel, 1990).

20. Psychological debriefing is a technique for providing emotional and psychological support immediately following a traumatic event. The goal of psychological debriefing is to prevent the development of PTSD and other mental health problems. Most psychological debriefing involves a single session, which might last between one and three hours, in the days immediately following a traumatic event.

Chapter 11

1. Philip S. Wang, Patricia A. Breglund, and Ronald C. Kessler, "Patterns and Correlates of Contacting Clergy for Mental Disorders in the United States," *Health Services Research* 38, no. 2 (2003): 647–673.

2. LifeWay Research, *Study of Acute Mental Illness and Christian Faith: Research Report*, 2014. Retrieved from http://lifewayresearch.com/mentalillnessstudy/.

3. Kay Warren speaking about Saddleback's Hope for Mental Health Community. Retrieved from kaywarren.com.

4. www.hopeandhealingcenter.org.